BORN TO DIE

BORN TO DIE

A COP KILLER'S FINAL MESSAGE

IAN MACDONALD
and
BETTY O'KEEFE

Heritage
House

National Library of Canada Cataloguing in Publication Data

Macdonald, Ian, 1928-
    Born to die: a cop killer's final message / Ian Macdonald and
Betty O'Keefe.

    Includes index.
    ISBN 1-894384-69-5

    1. Gordon, Joe, d. 1957. 2. Murderers—British Columbia—
Vancouver—Biography. 3. Vancouver (B.C.). Police Dept.—History.
I. O'Keefe, Betty, 1930-   II. Title.

HV6535.C23V345 2003   364.15'23'092   C2003-910979-8

First edition 2003

Heritage House acknowledges the financial support for our pub-
lishing program from the Government of Canada through the Book
Publishing Industry Development Program (BPIDP), Canada
Council for the Arts, and the British Columbia Arts Council.

Cover and book design by Marketing Dynamics
Layout by Darlene Nickull
Edited by Terri Elderton

HERITAGE HOUSE PUBLISHING COMPANY LTD.
Unit #108 – 17665 66A Ave., Surrey, BC V3S 2A7

Printed in Canada

BRITISH
COLUMBIA
ARTS COUNCIL
We acknowledge the support of the Province of British Columbia
through the British Columbia Arts Council

The Canada Council | Le Conseil des Arts
for the Arts | du Canada

DEDICATION

This book is dedicated to the members of the police department who have given their lives in the service of the City of Vancouver.

ACKNOWLEDGEMENTS

Thanks to retired Vancouver Police Inspector Ian Sinclair, to whom we are particularly indebted for providing photographs and sharing with us memories of his father and the incidents surrounding his father's death. We also thank retired Inspector Sid Devries for providing us with the facts about the quick apprehension of Joe Gordon.

Research assistants were Sheena Macdonald, Vancouver, and Vera Lucas, Victoria.

Other sources of information included the *Vancouver Daily Sun*, the *Vancouver Daily Province*, the *Vancouver News Herald*, the *New Westminster Columbian*, the *Victoria Colonist* and the *Victoria Times*. Names of the first two newspapers were later changed to *The Vancouver Sun* and *The Province*. Both the *News Herald* and the *Columbian* no longer publish, and the two Victoria papers have amalgamated into one, the *Times Colonist*.

" ... we taught our children
to be delinquents ... "

CONTENTS

PREFACE

It was a final message from a man in a prison cell on death row; he entitled it "Born to Die." And its purpose was carefully explained.

"Whatever good I can do before I depart this world of pain and tears let me do now ... so that whatever joy and happiness I may bring can in some measure replace the sufferings that others may feel."

Before he died, Joe Gordon made a plea to parents of the 1950s to provide the kind of family life he had never experienced. He had lived what he considered a wasted life. He was an intelligent man who read a great deal, but still could do nothing to change his own lifestyle and avoid the gallows. He had glimpsed the possibilities from afar, but in his 30-odd years, a happy family life, a place of love, warmth, comfort, and forgiveness, had always eluded him. Instead, he had settled for the excitement of the underworld, a quick fix, booze, false friendships, and bravado.

He heard his sentence of death in a chilly courtroom after one of the most sensational murder trials in the history of Vancouver, British Columbia, one that revealed the evil, violent underworld that flourished at a time of widespread local police corruption. It was an era when bomb blasts and gunfire echoed throughout Joe Gordon's city.

Few hardened criminals have left as thoughtful and considered an explanation of what happened to drag them into oblivion as did Joe Gordon, and so his words carry weight even 50 years after he wrote them. While circumstances in the downtown east side have changed in half a century, largely for the worse, his words are particularly relevant in view of attempts being made at the beginning of the 21st century to somehow improve the area where Joe Gordon's fate took shape. This brutal section of Vancouver, long scarred by addiction, hopelessness, and poverty, will continue to spawn Joe Gordons unless someone heeds his words.

Gordon's East Hastings Street was brash and bright with neon, bustling with people, a sassy, thumb-in-your-eye kind of place with an excitement all its own, reminiscent of the gangster era of the 1920s in the United States. At the time, it vied with lower Granville near the bridge over False Creek as the centre of after-hours clubs and hangouts, many of them operating illegally. When Joe Gordon walked these streets, they were still part of the city, not the abhorrent ghetto they have since become.

In the interim, the first few blocks of East Hastings in the downtown east side have become a slimy, barren slum where there are more drugs and more heartbreak than ever before. It is home to a mixture of people who for one reason or another still gravitate to this now sad and seedy place: the drug dealers who make their living off unfortunates around the city, the social welfare workers who face an impossible task marked by few successes, and the police who must focus on keeping death and property damage to a minimum.

Still, some of Joe's words about the kind of person who is attracted to such a place are as relevant today as they were when he wrote them. Joe's message took many hours to write. It was based on his personal experiences, his understanding of human behaviour gleaned from the criminals who were his friends, and the scholars whose books he read while he was in jail. Joe Gordon finished his letter only a day or two before April 2, 1957, more than a year after the brutal slaying of a policeman. He asked his lawyer to see that it was published in the newspapers should his desperate last-minute appeal to Ottawa for leniency fail. His last words brought little response from Vancouver officials at the time.

This is his story.

A LIFE OF CRIME

THE PATH OF JUVENILE DELINQUENCY IS BUT A STEP FROM THE
ROAD OF CRIME AND THAT TWISTING, TORTUOUS LANE OF
UNFORTUNATE HUMANS WHO WALK BY NIGHT, THE LEPERS OF
SOCIETY. FOR SOME IT IS A MEANS OF EXPERIENCE, FOR
OTHERS A CAREER. LIVE DANGEROUSLY AND DIE YOUNG.

—*Excerpt from Joe Gordon's final message*

Joe Gordon lived in two worlds, neither of them very attractive.
He spent a lot of time in jail, and the rest of the time he roamed
East Hastings Street or Granville Street by the bridge, often
dropping in at one of his favourite haunts, one of the dank dungeons
that served up the brew he preferred. This was where the enigma
that was Joe Gordon planned and plotted his next move, picked up
some change playing pool, or, when he was feeling lucky, sought out
a serious game of poker.

Joe was a committed criminal, always confident that the next heist
would be the big one. He was not, however, a particularly competent
crook. He'd spent much of his teenaged years and young adult life
in jail because his schemes failed and the law stepped in. Much of
the knowledge he had acquired he learned in jail. Vancouver's police
department much preferred to see him behind bars rather than out
on the streets causing grief for them. For Gordon, the police were
the enemy, the symbol of authority that often rankled, and he liked
to put one over on them whenever possible, be it a prank or a
punishable crime.

Despite his chosen lifestyle, Gordon was a handsome, likeable, outgoing young man. His cohorts and associates admired his devil-may-care attitude, the flamboyant way he dressed, the stories he could tell, and his familiarity with guns. Gordon revelled in their adulation, never admitting that he was more loser than winner in his life of crime, and there were only a very few who knew that Gordon had a mean streak that could explode into violence if he felt cornered or trapped.

Gordon's world, Vancouver's skid row, has sunk much lower than it was in his day. Although physically it was located in almost the same few blocks as it is now, in the 1950s drug use was limited and had not soared out of control. There were no stumbling, pathetic addicts injecting themselves openly in alleys and doorways; they fed their habits in private back rooms often supplied by the dealers themselves. Stores along Hastings with huge neon signs catered to families from across the city. There were groceries, meat stores, and the Army and Navy Department Store, which did a roaring trade. Restaurants served everything from liver and bacon to steak and onions, and the Only made the best clam chowder in town, its 30 stools and the large sign proclaiming NO WASHROOMS ensuring a quick turnover.

Gordon's downtown east side was much safer than it is today, but still populated by the down and out, the misfits of society. His buddies were generally drunks, derelicts, bookies, hookers, petty crooks, hustlers, and young Native people, particularly Native women from remote reserves, intrigued by what they thought were the exciting big-city bright lights. They all lived a hand-to-mouth existence, some better at it than others.

The neighbourhood in the late 1940s and 1950s was also infested with police informants involved in a dangerous game but desperate enough for money to sell anything for a shorter sentence or a bus or train ticket out of town. On the street, being labelled a rat meant being totally ostracized at best, and death for the informant at worst, but there were a few people desperate enough to play the stool-pigeon game.

The police kept a close eye on their clientele and listened to the constant scuttlebutt as they observed the scene and marched into dark smoky pubs to break up drunken fisticuffs. In mid-1955 the police themselves were in trouble, and because of it were often the butt of some rough-and-ready jokes on skid row. One of Joe Gordon's delights during the summer of 1955 was to mention the name of the then-infamous former chief of police, Walter Mulligan, who had recently fled the country rather than face prosecution for accepting bribes. A Royal Commission of Inquiry into the Vancouver Police Department's alleged corruption began in July of 1955. This crowd felt it was hilarious that the chief and some of his senior men had been found just as crooked as the criminals they were supposed to keep on the straight and narrow. When the cops entered a pub, the conversation often switched to a loud mention of payoffs and bribe-taking superintendents.

The drinking dives of East Hastings were originally an offshoot of British Columbia's archaic and incomprehensible liquor laws. They catered to tough, hard-drinking men from forest and mining camps around the province, who came to town with pocketfuls of money, hungry to have a good time. Vancouver had gone from being a bare-knuckle, hard-living, boisterous frontier town and seaport to the opposite extreme: a straight-laced, strictly regulated society with tightly clamped liquor laws. The churchgoing majority wanted it that way. The new government of Premier W.A.C. (Wacky) Bennett, like others before it, railed against the evils of drink in any form, but raked in as much tax money as it could from its sale in government-owned stores. Unfortunately, the system encouraged bootleggers, and there was a multitude of them operating profitably, if illegally, in after-hours joints, selling liquor-store products as well as their own bathtub concoctions. When the police turned a blind eye to the practice, operators soon branched into other shady activities.

At this time Vancouver had no cocktail bars, only beer parlours with segregated sections for men and for ladies and escorts—with strict rules about the height of the partitions that separated them. An association of hotel owners who liked being the only ones in town with a licence to sell beer legally didn't want anything to change, so it constantly lobbied to retain the status quo. At ten cents a glass, a Niagara of beer roared through the city every day, with no food allowed to lessen or slow its impact. There were some private clubs and a few dance halls like the Commodore Ballroom on Granville where—by various means—owners circumvented the law for a price, and the young, uptown set could sip drinks of their choice while listening to the sophisticated piano stylings of the Artic Club's talented Chris Gage, the songs of Eleanor Collins, or the orchestra of Dal Richards at the Panorama Roof. But only the music and the food were legal.

Another government regulation required that beer parlours close for an hour at dinnertime to encourage after-work drinkers to return to the bosoms of their families to get something to eat. The Lotus Hotel just across the road from the *Vancouver Daily Sun*, on the edge of Gordon's world, perhaps best exemplified the difference between uptown and the other side of town. It had a unique way of cleaning the establishment and maximizing the take. The Lotus had a slanted stone floor, so while the patrons were gone, staff simply hauled out a hose and washed it down. The tiles also took a toll on those who quaffed too many ten-centers and fell off their stools with head-rattling thumps. The drunk, semi-conscious, or totally besotted were then unceremoniously tossed out onto the sidewalk, including the odd scribe from the *Sun*.

One other outlandish provincial regulation added to the gloom. Pub windows were painted a dark colour in order to prevent passers-by from seeing in and wanting to join the happy throng inside. This meant that police often had to wander inside in order to observe the clientele. Allowing pedestrians to see the interior would have been a better deterrent to this swinging lifestyle. It's doubtful the sight would have enticed many to enter. Pubs of this era often stank of stale beer sopped up by soggy carpets, and tabletops frequently glistened with great pools of spillage. The furniture was chipped, scarred, and battered. Dim lighting barely penetrated the acrid pall of smoke blown from thousands of cigarettes and cheap, smelly cigars in this era when almost every patron puffed away, unaware of the consequences.

This was postwar boom time in Vancouver. There was a job for everyone who wanted it, and the growing forest industry, which provided half of the provincial government's income, was opening new mills all along the coast. The supply of timber seemed everlasting, new mines were being developed, and every day men arrived in town looking for a job or a way to spend their money. The seas and rivers provided salmon in abundance, although there were already warnings that more care was needed to ensure overfishing did not deplete stocks. There was only one dark cloud that couldn't be ignored. Crime was on the rise and getting more violent. Illegal drugs were becoming more plentiful and more varied, adding an increased dimension to the breaking of law and order.

As crime statistics got worse, Vancouver's population relied on its three daily papers for all its news. Radio played a minor role, and television was in its infancy. The *Vancouver Daily Sun* led the field in crime reporting, while the *Vancouver Daily Province* was more staid, carrying the slogan "Vancouver's family newspaper." The small-circulation *Vancouver News Herald*'s main preoccupation was trying to sell enough papers to stay alive. It folded a few years later.

One ace reporter on the *Sun* was the late Jack Webster, the haggis-voiced, irascible Scot who went on to national fame as a radio-hotline broadcaster and television personality. The *Sun* sent him underground to live for a week on skid row and mingle with its denizens. Residents were voicing increased concern because the police seemed unable to do anything about pervasive, illegal gambling; they soon would know the reason why. This is what Webster told the paper's readers, without any reference to the mounting drug crime and the increasing use of guns and other violence as old and new gangs fought turf wars for the lucrative trade. He wrote:

> "Hundreds of professional gamblers operate in the city, many of them taking part in illegal games—mostly poker—which take place after hours in city clubs, phony sports clubs and plain illegal joints—bookmakers, their employees, touts and runners operate in beer parlours, cigar stores, hotel lounges, taxi offices and what amounts to open 'betting

halls' ... bootleggers, free from competition from any all-night liquor stores, supply liquor freely on telephone orders, sell it to personal callers and even dish it up by the glass in private lounges."

This was Joe Gordon's world, a wide-open, roaring twenties-style Vancouver, filled with bright lights and excitement in addition to society's misfits and those anxious to exploit and plunder for profit. The weaker the police department, the easier and more lucrative was the game they all played.

JAUNTY JOE

JUVENILE DELINQUENCY BEGINS IN THE HOME AND EXPANDS
ON THE STREET ... IT CAN RESULT FROM THE INCOMPATIBILITY
OF PARENTS AND THE CHILD.

—*Excerpt from Joe Gordon's final message*

Within hours of his release from jail in March 1955, Joe Gordon was back on East Hastings Street, checking out some of his favourite hangouts: the New Dodson, the Balmoral, the Beacon, and the Regent. The Hastings strip from Carrall to Main was Gordon's turf. He knew all the owners of little cafés and the waiters who served beer behind the blacked-out windows. He had been away awhile, but little had changed. He stopped to buy cigarettes at a tiny smoke shop. He was greeted warmly and welcomed back by the owner before he placed a bet on a Saturday horse race. Murray Goldman's Menswear was only two blocks down the street, and Gordon dropped in to buy a new shirt. As he left the haberdashery he checked his image in a pawnshop window and then went looking for a room for the night. The first hotel was full. Two dozen loggers had just checked in. Gordon smiled. Loggers parted with a lot of money fast when they came to town, and he might by one means or another be able to get his hands on some of it. He was pretty good at pool, and his card game was well above average.

In the Strathcona, he recognized a couple of fellow cons and joined them at a table in the rear. There were rumours afoot and the

Murray Goldman's, where Joe Gordon bought his shirts, was located next door to the Daily Province *building at Hastings and Cambie streets. Sally Shops and Copps Shoes were in the same block, which was anchored by Woodwards department store, located farther east at the corner of Hastings and Abbott. Joe Gordon's favourite drinking places were just a couple of blocks down the street.*

latest exploits of the police department were the topic of discussion. One member of the company had been arrested and roughed up by two of the beat cops. He sported a black eye and was asking for suggestions about his best defence when he appeared in court. Gordon bought a round and the crowd at the table began to grow. Some of the bookies who paid protection money were sweating it out, as public knowledge of the payoffs they made to police began to spread. Gordon was pleased to learn that his pal at the tobacco shop was in the clear, so far. Gordon's ex-con cronies and fair-weather friends packed his table. They were surprised to see that Gordon was not low on funds and had picked up some ready cash somewhere. He was a big spender when he had money, and he loved the adulation given him by those who shared his wealth.

Apart from the enticement of his offer of free beer, Gordon was also a great talker, a teller of tall tales about his experiences in everything from small jails and lockups to the penitentiary, as well as important incidents in his part of town. His vocabulary extended well beyond the four-letter verbal limitations of much of his audience. Although they all knew Gordon was a graduate only of the school of hard knocks, his cohorts accorded him a certain respect because of his record and the years he had spent in jail. In the view of the regulars, Gordon was fearless, a great guy, and a smart crook. It was a reputation he revered.

Another reason for his position of prestige, the thing that made him stand out from his generally bedraggled beer-drinking buddies, was the dapper way he dressed. Gordon's suits weren't the finest worsted—they were the cheaper off-the-rack variety—but they were always well cleaned and pressed with razor-sharp creases in the pants. He liked black because it accentuated his dark hair and eyes, and he favoured big-brimmed fedora hats, worn at a jaunty angle. It was all designed to polish his successful gangster image. For special occasions he had at least one sports coat that was a bright plum colour. In plum, he was more apt to be on a date or out dancing than talking with the boys in the pub. Good-looking Gordon was quite the ladies' man and often was seen in the company of attractive young women. He was a trim, slightly built 135 pounds, about 5 feet 8 inches tall, and he had curly dark brown—nearly black—hair. When not playing the flamboyant man about town, Gordon could appear more studious or businesslike when he wore his horn-rimmed glasses. It all depended on his objective at the time. Although beer parlours were his favourite haunts, he wasn't a great drinker, and although possession of drugs had got him into trouble with the law, he was not a hardened junkie.

At the age of 32, Gordon was a complex man. He was born in Montreal, but had lived most of his life in Vancouver. The Gordons were a Jewish family, but Gordon seldom if ever attended synagogue services with them. He had four older brothers and three older sisters, and it appears he was at the end of the line for care and affection. His father, Charles Gordon, had served in the military in Italy and was an extremely strict disciplinarian. He demanded instant obedience and meted out corporal punishment if he didn't get it. Gordon was often on the receiving end of his wrath, being beaten with a strap at the slightest excuse. Gordon's mother, unfortunately, found her eighth child to be one too many and resented the trouble he caused. She also took some abuse from her husband, and the Gordon marriage eventually ended in divorce, but that was long after the couple's youngest son was kicked out to fend for himself.

Juvenile authorities first picked up Gordon when he ran away from home shortly after the Gordon family arrived in Vancouver. He was only six years old and was miserable as he tried to cope with his first year of school. The police found Gordon shortly after he was reported missing and took him to the station, but his father knowingly left him there overnight "to teach him a lesson." It was a terrifying experience. Gordon spent the night with drunks and drug addicts, and he never forgot how afraid he was. When he got home he was beaten again. He never forgave his father. His assertions about his father were later verified by acquaintances who had known Charlie Gordon. Charlie had a good record in his army service in Italy during the Second World War, but was a hard, difficult man. "I could go even further and say he was a real jerk, somebody you'd just as soon not know," one man said.

Gordon maintained that his father had thrashed him unmercifully even before the move to Vancouver, and he could not understand why the faults of his siblings were often ignored. From the age of six onward he was constantly in trouble. Three times before he was twelve years old he was sentenced to the Boys' Industrial Home, and each time he learned more about crime. The other young misfits readily accepted him and soon became his friends. By then, his mother refused to allow him back in the house, so he was out on the street on his own for good. At thirteen he was sentenced for the first time to Oakalla Prison Farm for possessing burglary tools, and it wasn't long before he had been convicted of everything from car theft to attempted robbery with violence, drug possession, and possession of an offensive weapon. All these things he had learned about from older boys at the detention centre. It was a formidable record, and it left little time for regular childhood activities. It is doubtful that Gordon showed up for school much after he was eight or nine; he was too busy learning to be a crook.

Although his formal education was skimpy, Gordon did have a thirst for knowledge and didn't waste all his years behind bars. He did a lot of reading from books in prison libraries, everything from potboilers to the classics and the writing of Greek philosophers from ancient times. Perhaps this was what set Gordon apart from his contemporaries and why his friends hung on his every word and believed it all. It was paradoxical, but when Gordon expounded on new ways to beat the system and to live the easy life, his cronies didn't see his dismal record of losses with the law as proof of failure. They believed they were listening to the words and views of a man who had committed his crimes and done his time, and who was now wise and experienced in ways they could only imagine. They didn't fully understand him, but they admired his philosophical approach to the ups and downs of life. They listened carefully. Gordon was a spellbinder, a super salesman who could have made a living at almost anything he chose, if he hadn't been a committed criminal.

His most recent release from the penitentiary marked the end of a six-year sentence imposed when Gordon was 24. He claimed he made a living in the following months as a gambler, although he had worked for a few weeks selling insurance on television sets and was listed in subsequent police reports as a salesman. But business was slow, and Gordon soon looked up an old buddy named Lawson who drove a cab and was willing, for a price, to wait for Gordon while he pulled a stick-up. Gordon often had one or two alternatives in mind when he called Lawson; the joints were well selected, and Gordon was in and out within minutes. Generally he was back at the gambling tables within a half hour.

Informants quickly let police know that Gordon was holding court in his old stomping grounds. Policemen on patrol knew that having an active Gordon on the crime scene was the last thing they needed, and they viewed him much differently than his cohorts. To them he was an unreformed, unrepentant, committed crook without any fear of the police. They assumed it would not be long before he was planning his next job, so they watched and waited. He would likely soon want more funds than a quick heist could supply. Perhaps they were tipped off, as after a few beers Gordon occasionally talked too much and too loudly.

The men pounding the beat were also interested in his new associate, a man who seemed to be a cut above the usual lowlifes of the area. This was Jimmy Carey. He, like Gordon, was a smooth talker who dressed well. Gordon had another new acquaintance; she was his most recent female conquest, a striking redhead who was only seventeen years old. Her name was Lillian Middlecoat. Lillian was a bit of a phenomenon in the underworld, a teenager with the assurance and sophistication of someone well beyond her years. She wasn't a hooker, although she kept some very rough company. Unlike the rest of Gordon's ne'er-do-well circle and his other girlfriends, she didn't have a criminal record, but police soon began quizzing their skid-row snitches about the girl and her relationship with Gordon. They didn't learn much. She was cautious and tight-lipped about her activities and her new boyfriend.

Rumours that Gordon was showing an interest in guns soon reached the street cops. Getting one was easy; there were lots of sources in Gordon's neighbourhood if one had the money. With the police department in turmoil and gang activity on the upswing, there was an increased demand for firepower. Prices for guns and ammunition were climbing, and this created even more tension for the stressed-out detectives and cops on the beat.

THE CITY'S FINEST

EVERY PERSON HAS CRIMINAL ELEMENTS WITHIN HIM—BUT
HE IS NOT BORN A CRIMINAL. MANY FACTORS GO INTO THE
RUINATION OF A PERSONALITY ...

—*Excerpt from Joe Gordon's final message*

By 1955 Vancouver's police department was looking at its 89th birthday, and it was not a happy one. The department was in turmoil as a result of the exploits of Police Chief Walter Mulligan. Over the years it had struggled through more than its share of disruption, upheaval, and scandal, not too unexpected for an organization always wide open to criticism from both the public and politicians. Police chiefs had come and gone; some lasted only a short time because of politics or incompetence, but never before had the department been exposed to such ridicule and derision as had become widespread when Police Chief Walter Mulligan fled the country in order to escape prosecution.

Forgotten were the heroics of the ten policemen who had died in the line of duty during the department's first 70 years. One of them was Chief of Police Robert McLellan, who had died leading a raid on an apartment to arrest a drug addict who had shot a small boy.

Now, not only had Walter Mulligan been pronounced corrupt and on the take, but numbers of his men in the gambling squad were under suspicion because of conflicting, unproven testimony given during an inquiry.[1] At this time, gambling, lotteries, and betting outside of the racetrack were all illegal. This led to a proliferation of cigar-store betting shops and backroom gambling halls. The long-lasting inquiry proved only that while policemen would always practise solidarity, many of them were unwilling to abide by the law and face the truth head on. Even the police union, formed in 1918 to fight for better wages and working conditions for the men and to act as a defensive mechanism and buffer between them and the politicians who sought a scapegoat for their own misadministration, could do little this time to help. Bribery and corruption had brought shame to the whole force. Two senior men had attempted suicide, one successfully—and he was less guilty than many others.

It had all begun nearly ten years earlier. There had been chiefs who were corrupt or incompetent, and sometimes both, but never before had the union and all the senior officers been as enraged as they were in 1946 when big, bluff Walter Mulligan jumped up the promotion ladder, passing many others with more experience to take the top post. Mulligan knew how to cozy up to those who counted and was handed the job by his pal, Mayor Gerry McGeer, who was also head of the police commission. He liked the 230-pound Irishman as much as the senior men he outdistanced disliked him. But Mulligan faced union hostility and opposition from the start, the official department history understating only that the union "never had much time for the new chief." Mulligan's efforts to modernize the department, many of them admired in other jurisdictions, were contested by the union and the men under his command. One of his most unpopular moves was the introduction of one-man patrol cars, which would soon be blamed for the murder of a well-liked and respected on-duty cop.

In the beginning there was no clear evidence of any wrongdoing in the department involving senior officers. Mulligan eschewed big cars, big houses, and boats and seemed to live modestly on his $10,000-a-year salary, low for the head of a 600-man department. The death of his friend and mentor McGeer only a year after his appointment left him high and dry with little political support, so he sometimes offered his services to high-ranking politicians as a guide to some of the better fun spots and gambling dens in Chinatown and the downtown east side. The police department's history explains: "Things started to fall apart for Chief Mulligan. Rumours began to circulate that he was too friendly with people involved in illegal gambling and there was major discontent within the department." The unhappy policemen, including many senior officers, were, of course, responsible for a lot of the rumours. Reporters on the police beat were passed some tasty tips, and they went digging to confirm some of them. This led to the events of June 24, 1955, when chaos at the police station brought everything tumbling down.

Newly aware that a scandal sheet was about to run a big exposé on a long-running protection racket, Detective Sergeant Len Cuthbert, head of the gambling squad, was alone in the squad room when he tried to kill himself with his service revolver. He was later revealed as a man who was Mulligan's accomplice, the one who collected pay-off money in brown paper bags from bookies, which he split with the chief. Cuthbert fired his gun into his chest, missed his heart and lived. He later testified at the royal commission hearings, suggesting that more than half of his gambling detail was on the take. In the witness stand, other officers denied everything and had an amazing lack of recall, some barely remembering their names.

The Royal Commission of Inquiry into the police department's alleged corruption began in July 1955 and continued for seven months. The commission became known as the Tupper Inquiry because it was headed by Reginald Tupper, Q.C., son of the well-known Canadian Sir Charles Tupper. As an intrigued and shocked public heard or read about the unfolding evidence, Mulligan's mistress appeared, heavily veiled, to tell her story. Soon everyone was asking what chance the war on crime had when the chief was a crook. Before his turn to testify, Mulligan fled to the United States. The commission's report found him corrupt, but there wasn't enough evidence to justify extradition. Mulligan worked in the United States for several years before quietly moving back to Victoria, B.C., where he died many years later. The commission's report and Mulligan's departure left the police department in turmoil, rudderless and, for the time being, ineffective. Its troubles were far from over, as it would be some time before a new chief could repair the dysfunctional force. In the meantime, Joe Gordon and his friends enjoyed their new status of equality with the cops on the beat.

GANGLAND MURDER

THE FUNDAMENTAL PRINCIPLE OF LIFE IS SELF-PRESERVATION.
YOU BLINDLY FOLLOW INSTINCT AND FIGHT WITH WHATEVER
MEANS AT YOUR COMMAND ... WILLFUL DESIRE AND
THOUGHTLESS EMOTION RULE.

—*Excerpt from Joe Gordon's final message*

Vancouver's mounting crime wave, which increased on the heels of the Mulligan Affair, was punctuated by gunfire, car bombings, bank robberies, and, on one occasion, by the screams of a small-time drug pusher when his legs were smashed by a mobster's iron bar. Battles between drug gangs for control of the burgeoning drug trade began to make newspaper headlines.

As the wars escalated during the summer months, public concern grew into fear, resulting in angry demands for something to be done quickly before the reputation of Canada's idyllic young city by the blue Pacific became hopelessly sullied. City hall fussed and fretted but seemed incapable of any decisive action to improve the situation. Some officials, as well as the public, began to question the honesty and integrity of the entire police force, which seemed to be deteriorating further as each day passed. Its tarnished reputation and the uncertainty about who had been involved with Mulligan and who was innocent had created a force whose morale ebbed away with each new unsolved case.

One of the flagrant front-page stories about violent crime bore the stamp of a Chicago-style execution. Danny Brent was a middleman. He got supplies from major drug dealers and passed them on to hustlers who moved the merchandise onto the streets. His career came to a brutal and abrupt end when he was taken for a deadly ride; his bullet-riddled body was found on a rain-swept fairway at the University Golf Club. One hardened, cynical cop quipped that Brent was dumped only a chip shot from the tenth green. The killers had stuffed newspapers inside their victim's clothing, presumably to stop blood from soiling the inside of their car as it was driven to the university district.

Brent's demise was the talk of the east side. One of Gordon's pals observed that it was the closest that Danny ever got to higher education. Brent, like Gordon, was a smooth, affable guy and head waiter at the Press Club, a private downscale dive for an assorted crowd that had nothing to do with newspaper people. In the dim, distant past, someone had conned the journalists out of their licence and the name Press Club, forcing them to adopt the title of Newsmen's Club of B.C. Danny was vice-president of the Press Club's labour union, Local 240 of the Club, Cabaret, and Construction Camp Culinary and Service Employees Union, a long and wonderful title for a fairly small group of people. He was, of course, also a drug dealer, and his funeral was something to behold. He lay in an open casket surrounded by a huge array of flowers and expensive wreaths—a display usually accorded a major hood or a mafia don. Despite the mortician's best efforts, a bullet hole on his face could not be completely disguised, and it was a shock for the bevy of girls from the club who attended his funeral and viewed his corpse. Police later found a large amount of heroin in a strongbox belonging to Brent, but they never came up with his killers despite the large reward offered by the club's owners.

Gordon and his east-side friends were also well acquainted with 51-year-old Bill Semenick; some had done time with him. Semenick was another drug dealer. He too had been taken for a ride, but he managed to jump from the car in a hail of bullets as he was being driven through Stanley Park, presumably on the way to find a quiet spot for his execution. Semenick had carefully chosen the spot to make a run for it, so when he spotted a police car on regular park patrol he took off like a jackrabbit. Bill Lindsay was the cop behind the wheel, a member of the department's regular mounted squad, and he knew the park like the palm of his hand. When the kidnappers saw the cop, they fled in the car in the opposite direction from the one taken by Semenick. It didn't take long for Lindsay and the crew who arrived to aid in the search to round up all three. One of the kidnappers was found some time later trying to hide, up to his neck in the cold waters of nearby Coal Harbour. Semenick acquired the nickname "Silent Bill," bestowed on him by the press when he refused to testify against the two accused. He already knew he was heading back to jail, because he was facing a trafficking charge. Now the law of the underworld prevailed. Flashy in gabardine suits and wide-brimmed fedoras, Eddie Sherban and Joe Marcoux, the accused kidnappers, both well known to police, smirked and laughed as they walked away from the courthouse with their girlfriends. Frustrated officials could only watch, knowing Sherban and Marcoux would continue to be a problem for them. Semenick got ten years on the trafficking charge, plus three months for refusing to testify.

Joe Gordon had shared the odd drink with another underworld character, Jack Leonhard, who created front-page headlines soon after Semenick. Leonhard's car was parked in his own driveway when he turned on the ignition and touched off a blast that shredded the automobile. The powerful explosion rattled the district for blocks around. Somehow Leonhard survived, although he lost a leg in the explosion. Police said he was a drug dealer, but he denied the claim, saying he had no idea why anybody would want to kill him. Police probed his links to the drug world but could not come up with enough evidence to bring the case to trial. The car bombing became just another unsolved crime in the long list.

Vancouver Mayor Fred Hume despaired of the increasing amount of crime-filled, harmful publicity the city was getting—hardly the stuff to attract tourists and conventions. Hume agreed with the media and linked the Brent Semenick–Leonhard incidents, promising swift and decisive action to "uproot gangland criminals." A prosperous businessman-cum-mayor who quailed at anything that could upset the quiet life and Vancouver's economy, Hume was now on the spot, trying to explain how Walter Mulligan could have gone so far astray and yet remain as the police chief so long without anybody noticing what was going on and stepping in to stop it. Hume was not only mayor, but also chairman of the three-man police commission that had approved Mulligan's promotion. Gerry McGeer was dead, so Hume was the obvious man to blame, and he was doing his best to get out from under what had become an embarrassing situation.

The atmosphere became so volatile in Vancouver that officialdom, the press, and the public began to look at crime and its causes in unusual ways. They complained about the sudden appearance on the entertainment scene of Elvis Presley, the swivel-hipped singer and new rock-and-roll idol. Why had Ed Sullivan allowed Presley to be seen only from the waist up when he appeared on his popular television show for the first time, they asked? Could Presley's gyrations affect the thoughts and behaviour of the young? In all seriousness, the Vancouver School Board pondered the question at a meeting, discussing whether this new rock-and-roll was a threat to the proper upbringing of the young, who, of course, loved it. Newspapers reported on the musings of assorted behavioural specialists, some of whom uttered nonsensical comments about rock-and-roll signifying "the end of civilization as we know it."

Apart from laughing and making jokes about the embarrassing hole the Vancouver Police Department had made for itself, restless Joe Gordon found he had a pressing problem to solve. He was finally running short of funds, and the discomfort of the city's finest did nothing to solve his looming problem. Gordon knew he was always "a man of interest" to the police, who knew his hangouts and often questioned his associates. He wasn't aware, however, of the link between his new pal, Jimmy Carey, and another force, the Royal Canadian Mounted Police (RCMP).

The predictions of the men on the beat that it was only a matter of time before Gordon would "mastermind" another job took seven months to materialize. Gordon's stash of cash and his wits had kept him well provided for until late October, when he found it necessary to pull a big job. On October 25, 1955, his new caper triggered a chain of events with tragic and fatal consequences.

BANK ROBBERY

PUNISHMENT SUCCEEDS VERY WELL IN MAKING CRIMINALS. IT
ALSO KEEPS YOU ON THE ROAD OF CRIME AND IN THE
COMPANY OF CRIMINALS.

—Excerpt from Joe Gordon's final message

Bank holdups had become an epidemic throughout the Lower Mainland. Each time one occurred a bell would clang on the police radio network, giving the address of the latest attempt and providing whatever information was immediately available. The ringing sent the nearest police cars racing to the scene with flashing lights and screaming sirens. Newspapers and radio stations also monitored the network and sent reporters, photographers, and cameramen rushing to get a story, although often the bell signalled a false alarm. The call on October 25 was the real thing: Robbers had struck the Bank of Commerce at 2884 Grandview Highway in the suburbs. By the time the first police car arrived on the scene, the holdup gang had fled.

Employees said that two armed, masked men had burst in just before 11:00 a.m. when the branch was quiet. They herded four staff members into a back room and at gunpoint ordered them to open the safe. When one young man didn't act quickly enough, he was struck on the head with a gun barrel but was not seriously hurt. After this incident the bank manager quickly opened the safe and watched as the robbers scooped up bills of every denomination and stuffed them into a metal box. The two bandits managed to grab

33

more than $26,000—much more than the usual haul. The gunmen then fled the bank, taking the manager's revolver with them. He had tried but had been unable to use it during the holdup. As the robbers disappeared through the door, manager J.E. Mennie hit the alarm button and the police came rushing, followed as always by cars full of media people.

Eyewitnesses told the first officers at the scene that a "beautiful" young woman was behind the wheel of the getaway car that roared away with tires screaming after the gunmen jumped in. One very alert passer-by had noted the licence-plate number; she gave it to police and the hunt was on. Several cars scouted the nearby streets while roadblocks were set up at main intersections. It didn't take long before the abandoned car was found. Not far away police saw a young woman who caught their interest as she walked hurriedly down the sidewalk. When they apprehended Catherine Pilling she gave up without a struggle; police found she was carrying a large sum of money. The case developed quickly. A young man, Henry Allan Clark, walked into the local police station shortly after the holdup and told a confusing story about his car being stolen. After some questioning his story fell apart, and he admitted that the car they had found abandoned was his. Clark contended he had loaned it to a friend, and he was immediately held as a material witness.

A few hours later the police arrested Joe Gordon in downtown Vancouver. He wasn't carrying a gun or any large amount of money and was picked up without incident. It was never stated publicly how the police were able to tie Gordon to the holdup and knew where to find him and make the arrest so quickly, but it was obvious that either Pilling or Clark had fingered him.

Joe Gordon appeared in court the next day and was his usual unflappable self. He almost seemed to enjoy the attention given him by lawyers and judges. The court was told he had no fixed address, and he was remanded on $15,000 bail. Even for someone with Gordon's record it was a fairly hefty sum. The two others accused paid lesser amounts. As he set bail, obviously believing that it was unlikely the accused could come up with that kind of money, Magistrate Oscar Orr uttered some prophetic words. He commented to Gordon's lawyer, Larry Hill, "It might be a good idea to keep people like this out of circulation." Sadly for a veteran policeman, his wife, and their three teenaged children, Gordon couldn't be held: There was some surprise in the courtroom when Gordon's lawyer was able to come up with the money. Whether it came from a stash that Gordon had hidden away—although it was believed he was short of funds before the bank holdup—or if it was put up by a friend was never divulged. Swaggering, confident, cocky, and increasingly dangerous, Joe Gordon was on the loose again.

CONSTABLE GORDON SINCLAIR

HOME ENVIRONMENT AND PARENTAL LOVE ARE BASIC IN THE DEVELOPMENT OF A CHILD.

—*Excerpt from Joe Gordon's final message*

By Vancouver standards, the evening of December 7, 1955, was a very bleak winter's night; the weatherman had predicted storm-whipped sleet or wet snow, and for once he was right. A fourteen-year veteran of the Vancouver Police Department with a wide variety of assignments under his belt, Gordon Sinclair rose from the dinner table and prepared to return to work. Because his current beat was close to home, he had taken his dinner break with his family. Recently the 41-year-old policeman had successfully completed examinations that put him in line for a promotion from first-class constable to sergeant.

A cheerful, outgoing, craggy-featured man, Gordon Sinclair was well known in the community and on the force as one of the leaders of the Vancouver Police Pipe Band, which played at many Vancouver events and was often requested to fill out-of-town engagements. A native of Brandon, Manitoba, Sinclair had been pipe major of the Brandon Boys Pipe Band, and when he took a job in Trail, B.C., he became pipe major of the Trail Pipe Band. He was a Celtic folklorist, an accomplished piper, a composer of pipe music, president of the B.C. Pipers' Association and much sought after in the Pacific Northwest for his experience on the bagpipes and his excellent teaching techniques.

A few days earlier, Sinclair's smiling face had appeared on the front page of the *Vancouver Sun*; he was supposedly showing Mayor Fred Hume and the Caledonian Society's president, George Gibson, how to play the bagpipes. The occasion was the official opening of the Scottish auditorium at Twelfth Avenue and Fir. Sinclair was a well-known member of the society. He was proud of his Scottish heritage and attended as many Scottish functions as he could crowd into his busy life. He and his family had recently competed at a Highland celebration in Seattle, Washington; he and his

Gordon Sinclair, pictured here wearing the uniform of the Vancouver Police Pipe Band, was a well-known piper. He taught the bagpipes to many youngsters who were enrolled in local bands.

son played the pipes and his two daughters competed in Highland dancing. Some of the Christmas presents that awaited him in three weeks' time had been bought during that visit. Neighbours often saw the close-knit family leaving on regular weekend trips to compete in Highland Games events in Seattle, Portland, Victoria, or other nearby cities.

The Sinclairs lived in a neat, well-kept, two-storey home on Vancouver's west side. His son Ian had days earlier celebrated his seventeenth birthday, and his daughters Aileen and Lynne were aged fourteen and twelve. They all attended Kitsilano High School, where their mother worked in the cafeteria as a pastry cook. Sinclair and his son Ian were also enthusiastic fishermen and often took off for a day or an evening of fishing in their sixteen-foot wooden-hulled boat that was kept at Fraser's Wharf in Kitsilano. On most occasions Lady, their faithful black retriever, accompanied them. Sinclair tried hard to fit in as many weekends away as he could. Somehow he also found time to be a skip in the

Gordon and Agnes Sinclair, with children Lynne, Aileen, and Ian, on the steps of their home at 2647 West 14th Avenue in 1949, just a few years before the shooting.

Police Mutual Benevolent Association curling club, where he threw a mean stone.

As he prepared to return to work that stormy December night, Sinclair joked with his oldest daughter Aileen and her friend Barbara Russell, who was also fourteen. The girls were close, and Barbara, who lived just across the street, was a frequent and welcome visitor in the Sinclair household. The policeman enjoyed teasing the girls, and they giggled as he commented with mock horror at the style of clothes they and their teenaged friends favoured. After a final check at his reflection in the hall mirror, he kissed his wife

Agnes on the cheek and said, "Goodbye, I'll see you in a little while." Sinclair was working the 4:00 p.m. to midnight shift in car number twelve. He worked out of Police Section Four at 42nd Avenue and West Boulevard and patrolled an area adjacent to where he lived. As he left the house it was just 6:30 p.m.

Agnes probably felt no foreboding as her husband departed for duty. Over the years she had learned not to worry too much, assured by her husband that he knew what he was doing. So far, he had escaped unscathed despite having spent much of his time working in the city's toughest areas. Recently, Sinclair had been a radio dispatcher, but now he had returned to patrol duty. His shift called for him to operate a one-man car in an area adjacent to downtown. Strong opposition to the practice of putting officers alone in patrol cars had been mounted by the police union, which argued for retention of the long-standing two-man system, particularly in the skid row area and some of the other trouble spots, like the dives near the Granville Street Bridge—well-known hangouts of thieves, addicts, traffickers, and other violent criminals. Sinclair and his colleagues knew well that the increasing use of guns in the city upped the risks, although few ever talked about this reality with their families.

There had been gunplay, but fortunately no fatalities in the Vancouver department since a vicious gun battle on False Creek on February 26, 1947, which claimed the lives of two policemen, Charles Boyce and Oliver Ledingham. When confronted by the pair, three young bank holdup suspects pulled out weapons and began firing at the patrolmen, who returned their fire. In the blazing gunfight that ensued, both Boyce and Ledingham were killed, along with one robber; another was hanged for the murders of the policemen, and one was found not guilty at trial.

Gordon Sinclair climbed into his car and drove into a dark, wet, cold winter's night that was steadily growing worse, brightened only by strings of coloured Christmas lights on storefronts and around some homes. He headed for his patrol area along West Fourth Avenue just south of the Granville Street Bridge.

SHOTS FIRED

YOU LEARN FROM THEM HOW TO STEAL A CAR, BREAK INTO ANY SORT OF DWELLING, BLOW OPEN A SAFE ... TO BECOME A DRUG CONNECTION AND A GUN MAN.

—*Excerpt from Joe Gordon's final message*

Jens Nielsen was a young Danish immigrant who lived with his wife and baby in an apartment at 1527 West Fourth. It was a semi-industrial area and a quiet place at night, when the business plants and commercial establishments were closed. His wife was in the basement laundry room getting fresh diapers when she looked out the window and saw two men apparently carefully checking the street to see if anyone was about. Their behaviour seemed furtive, raising her suspicions, and she watched as they turned toward the darkened office of a fuel-supply company across the street. There they crouched, huddled together, smoking, occasionally conversing, and keeping an eye on the street. She wondered what they had in mind and if they might be burglars. When one of them put on white gloves, she became more suspicious. She continued to watch as they walked over to a car parked with its lights turned off in an alley about 100 yards away. The two men then walked back toward the office building and peered into the darkened window again.

Mrs. Nielsen hurried upstairs to tell her husband what she had seen. He looked out of the apartment window and could easily see the two men across the street. As he watched, one of them put on what looked like a mask. The area was poorly lit, partly hidden by one of the off ramps from the Granville Street Bridge at Third Avenue. Police headquarters' records noted that it was exactly 6:39 p.m. when they received a phone call from Nielson. He reported seeing prowlers and explained what he and his wife had witnessed. Sinclair was cruising nearby when the radio message was relayed from the station to look for prowlers possibly casing the Watkins Winram plant in his area. Two other policemen, Derek Brookes and Hugh Wiebe, were on patrol in a two-man traffic car farther up Granville Street. They heard the radio dispatcher send Sinclair to the scene and immediately sped to provide backup for their fellow officer. When they asked for confirmation of the address, Sinclair replied he was almost at the scene.

While the police moved in, Nielsen watched from his window. He saw Sinclair drive along Third Avenue, turn around at the corner, and then head back toward the plant. The policeman swung his car over to the wrong side of the street, where his headlights illuminated the scene. Nielsen's view was obscured at this point. He later told reporters, "Then I heard two or three bangs. I'm not sure how many. I thought it was a car backfiring." Anxious to see what was happening, he dashed outside just in time to observe a man running across a vacant lot, with a policeman in hot pursuit. He said the policeman shouted, "Come and help." The young father halted briefly in his recital of events to reporters, looking shamefaced as he confessed that he turned down the policeman's call for help. He said he was terrified when he realized the noise he had heard wasn't a car backfiring but actually the sound of gunfire. "I didn't want to get shot," Nielsen stated.

Brookes and Wiebe hadn't seen Sinclair's car when they first arrived at the plant about a minute and a half after he confirmed the address. They had stopped behind the office building, where Brookes saw a man racing off in frantic flight, stumbling as he negotiated the rough ground of an adjacent vacant lot. Brookes leapt out of the car and gave chase on foot as the man sped up, increasing his lead on the pursuing cop. Almost at the same time, Wiebe gunned the cruiser and took off after a convertible that had suddenly appeared—with tires screaming—from an adjacent alley. He had to make a U-turn to give chase, but he saw the convertible skid to a halt at Fir and Fifth Avenue, where two men appeared out of the shadows and jumped in. Within seconds the car roared off again. Wiebe took up the pursuit to Fir and Eighth Avenue, where he caught up with the fleeing vehicle and attempted to pass it and cut it off. As he pulled alongside, the car stopped suddenly; two men jumped out and disappeared into the night. As Wiebe skidded to a halt, the convertible backed up around the intersection and raced off again, quickly getting lost in traffic on Broadway. The officer knew it was useless to resume the chase, so he radioed in a description of the vehicle as he returned to the Watkins Winram plant.

Meanwhile, another nearby resident, Gordon Goll, who had seen Sinclair's car parked on the wrong side of the street with its lights blazing, the engine running, and the driver's door wide open, realized something was wrong and ran over to investigate. He saw a policeman lying beside the cruiser and almost immediately noticed Brookes returning to the scene after losing sight of the fleeing suspect he had chased across the vacant lot and through the dark streets. Goll, shocked by the sight of the policeman lying in the street, yelled fearfully for Brookes to hurry over. Sinclair was on the ground, his head in the gutter, with one foot still inside the car. His cap lay beside him and his gun was still in its holster. He lay in a spreading pool of his own blood and appeared to be dead.

Brookes leaned through the open door of Sinclair's cruiser and used the radio to put through a call for help. "Send an ambulance," he told headquarters. "For God's sake, hurry!" He could see blood oozing from Sinclair's head, soaking the back of his tunic. By the time wailing sirens announced the arrival of the ambulance, police throughout the Lower Mainland were racing across town toward the scene of the crime. They were ignited to action by the chilling news broadcast on the police radio: "Policeman down." Almost immediately, detectives ordered roadblocks thrown up throughout the area. All cars were stopped and drivers questioned about the convertible.

Within minutes, off-duty policemen were turning up at westside stations and at the scene of the shooting, ready to help with what was to become a massive manhunt. In the meantime, Wiebe had located the building where a man had been seen running toward the rear exit. At the entrance to the apartment he found a .45 revolver lying on the ground. It didn't seem to have been fired, but he immediately turned it over to detectives. As the hunt intensified, Mayor Hume offered his official car to help in the search. He was attending a meeting of the police commission when the news about Sinclair's shooting was relayed to him.

While some investigators combed the scene, the grounds of the plant, and the vacant lot next door, others headed for skid row and its well-known criminal hangouts to track down any informants who might know something about the attempted break-in and shooting. About this time, a terse message that many hoped they wouldn't hear went out over the police radio. It confirmed the worst fears of every man on the force. An unemotional voice stated, "All cars: PC 246 was DOA at VGH." Gordon Sinclair had been pronounced dead at the emergency room at Vancouver General Hospital. The family man, the popular policeman, and piper, had died in the service of his city from gunshot wounds to the head and body, murdered by an as yet unknown killer. As he watched, the young carpenter Nielsen sadly expressed regret to reporters and cameramen who had flocked to the scene: "I'm sorry I telephoned police. If I hadn't, the officer might still be alive."

THE HUNT INTENSIFIES

NO ONE IS ENTIRELY GOOD OR ENTIRELY BAD. WE ALL EXCUSE OUR OWN FAILURES BUT SELDOM, IF EVER, DO WE EXCUSE THE FAILURES OF OTHERS.

—*Excerpt from Joe Gordon's final message*

Nothing stirs a police department faster or reaches the intensity of the drive mounted by any force, even one in bad shape, than the hunt for a cop killer. Vancouver's lawmen had been demoralized, some ashamed of their recent less-than-encouraging record, but now they had a duty to a fellow officer to find his killer. All their efforts were instantly concentrated on one thing: finding the men involved in the slaying of Gordon Sinclair. There were now no questions and no arguments. Every man on the force had the same objective: to bring the perpetrators to justice.

As soon as the awful news was heard on police-car radios, brusque orders were barked out at roadblocks along Fourth Avenue as the interrogation of motorists spread throughout the Kitsilano district. Every car was searched while patrols crept silently down the dark streets. It didn't take long for the first break in the case. The 1953 convertible getaway car was found about 10:00 p.m., parked in the 1900-block West Seventh, not too far from the scene of the killing. Police attention was drawn to it because of the sloppy way it had been parked, with the rear of the vehicle sticking out into the street. A quick licence check showed it was owned by a criminal who had been in jail since October, serving a nine-month term for possession of stolen goods. He was immediately questioned and said he had loaned the car to a friend while he was in prison. Police found and questioned the friend, a well-known bootlegger, who said he had left it earlier in the day parked in the 1400-block West Pender with the keys in the glove compartment.

As the police interrogated him, he kept repeating, "I didn't kill the guy." He wouldn't say if he had loaned the car to a friend, but it was obvious he had, and the police knew that one of his close cohorts was Joe Gordon. Gordon had been unusually quiet since getting out of jail, but police had been waiting for him to pull another job. This could be it. Joe Gordon almost immediately became a suspect in the aborted break-in and killing. As police quizzed more witnesses and fitted the facts together, he became more than just a possible suspect, and the hunt for him intensified.

Mrs. Edna Vachyinsky, who lived near the Watkins Winram plant, confirmed the Nielsens' account. She said she saw a car drive slowly up the lane near the plant, dim its lights, and stop. She watched as two men got out. Others said they heard shots and some stated they heard a crashing sound. Police found a piece of broken fencing lying on the lawn of a nearby house and identified it as the possible source of the noise. They suspected it had been destroyed when one of the fleeing gunmen smashed into it in his desperate effort to escape. A ten-year-old boy who had been playing nearby told police he heard a shot and then saw a policeman chasing another man. "It didn't look so nice so I ran home," he said.

Henry Peters, sixteen, was stunned when he learned he had confronted a possible killer. The teenager said he had met a man running through the hallway of a nearby rooming house at 1067 West Fifth, where he was visiting his relatives. Young Peters said the man was flushed and panting, but still took time to say, "Hi," as he charged down the corridor. Peters saw him trip and fall, but, apparently unhurt, he got up quickly and raced out the back door. "He was scared of something," Peters told reporters. "He just wanted to get out of there in a hurry."

The detective squad developed the theory that Sinclair had recognized one of the suspected robbers as soon as he pulled up and moved to get out of the cruiser, so the gunman, rather than be caught in the act, shot first. Police reiterated that the recognition factor was probably why a second bullet had been fired into Sinclair's back after he fell beside the cruiser, downed by the first shot. The killer wanted to be sure Sinclair was dead and could not identify him. There were scattered reports that Sinclair had died with his hand on his gun, but this was just one of many rumours. He had had no opportunity to pull his revolver. It was in his holster when he fell. The shooting had happened too fast for Sinclair to retaliate. An anguished Constable Brookes expressed the feelings of all the men involved in the hunt: "He didn't have a chance, the poor guy."

Acting Chief Alan Rossiter had the job of delivering the sad news to Mrs. Agnes Sinclair and her family. Afterwards, the shaken policeman said that despite the terrible suddenness of her husband's death, she had taken the news very well. As he left, however, and as relatives and friends arrived, Agnes Sinclair burst into tears and sobbed, "They never gave him a chance. They just shot him through the head. There will never be another man for me. There was only one, Gordon, and he's gone now." A doctor was called and said Mrs. Sinclair had suffered severe shock.

Sinclair's older daughter, Aileen, was consoled by her friend Barbara Russell, who had been kibitzing with the policeman only twenty minutes before his death. Aileen wondered how the family could face Christmas without him, and Barbara called Sinclair her second dad. She said, "He was like a father to me ever since my mother and I moved up here. He was about the same age my father would be. My father died when I was eleven months old."

Detectives used inducements and threats as they worked their way through the underworld looking for suspects and for Joe Gordon in particular. Informants and stoolies were squeezed hard, but in the end it was a lucky break that led to the arrest of Gordon. The drug squad's Sid Devries had kept an eye on Gordon because of his association with key men in the drug trade and had jotted down the licence-plate number of a car he saw Gordon driving. When the plate number of the abandoned getaway car was relayed to headquarters, Devries identified it immediately as the vehicle

Gordon had been driving. Other officers who had been keeping an eye on Gordon knew of an address at which he sometimes stayed, and shortly before midnight police raided an apartment at 1350 Burrard Street, not too far from the scene of the shooting. They were prepared for trouble and possibly gunplay, but there was none. They arrested Joe Gordon and four others who were in the suite at the time. They were a 37-year-old mechanic, a 22-year-old logger, a 19-year-old woman, and a youth. No weapons were found. A search of the apartment revealed only one interesting item: a small parcel wrapped in brown paper that Gordon admitted was his. It contained a pair of brown shoes and a pair of pants, both well spattered with mud. Everyone in the apartment was arrested and taken to police headquarters for questioning, while the brown bag and its contents were turned over to the police laboratory for examination.

With the arrest of the five at the Burrard Street apartment, police officers had difficulty disguising their belief that they had the murderers in custody. Joe Gordon, true to his reputation, stayed calm, cool, and tight-lipped about everything, except that he vehemently insisted he wasn't the killer and he denied that he had been anywhere near the scene of the slaying. Throughout the night investigators grilled him, as well as the others picked up at the apartment, without results.

While detectives continued to question Gordon, senior officers and city officials held a hurriedly called meeting. The grim-faced policemen made it clear they were determined to show the underworld that a constable couldn't be brutally murdered without someone paying the price for it. The evidence they had gathered included a crude white cloth mask discovered on the grounds of the plant, a gun found in the yard of the nearby apartment building, a plaster cast of a footprint taken at the scene, a parcel containing dirty shoes and clothing—and they also had Joe Gordon. They were sure he was the killer. Now all they had to do was prove it.

Acting Chief Rossiter was confident enough to tell reporters a few hours later, "We believe we have the right man." He didn't name him, but reporters knew who he was. Rossiter added that the man was in custody and was a well-known criminal with a long record.

Ballistics tests had already shown that the .45 recovered at the scene was not the one that fired the fatal shots, although it likely was carried to the scene by one of the suspects, Rossiter said. He also revealed that, in response to the incident, he had beefed up some downtown patrols into two-man operations.

Word spread quickly through the underworld that Gordon was being held for the cop killing. No one was aware, however, that the Nielsens, eyewitnesses to the slaying and now under police protection, had failed to identify Gordon as one of the holdup men. Investigators were very unhappy that they didn't have the confirmation they needed to put Gordon at the scene.

In the public domain, angry accusations began to surface, hurled against police headquarters in particular, and ex-police chief Mulligan was roundly cursed on a number of occasions. Of course, he wasn't there to hear them. Police-union boss Detective Fred Dougherty was particularly incensed, repeating his earlier denunciations of the ex-chief's introduction of the one-man patrol-car system. Dougherty said there was no doubt Sinclair would be alive if two men had answered the call. Passion ran high, but privately some disagreed with the union leader's angry views. They weren't enamoured of the policy, but they didn't think it was the sole reason for Sinclair's murder. They said that in a two-man operation, one officer would have left the car at the back of the building and one would have gone around to the front with the cruiser. He would have run into a gunman at the front as Sinclair did. All of it was speculation, but Rossiter's early comment that he didn't think the policy had much to do with the killing didn't please many of his men.

Shaken Mayor Fred Hume immediately put up $1,000 of his own money as a reward for finding the killer or killers and began to try to separate himself from the one-man car issue. He stated that despite being the police-commission chairman he had never liked the policy and had gone along with it on Mulligan's recommendation, regarding the chief as the expert on the subject. Nearly everyone stressed that it was totally Mulligan's idea and responsibility, but there is no doubt the proposed policy could have been turned down by the commission had it wanted to do so. Commissioners were all aware of the opposition to the policy within the department.

One of many public statements made about the one-man patrol system came from top-ranking labour leader and alderman Bert Showler. The respected 65-year-old civic politician had held decided views about Mulligan's policy from the outset, when it first came under fire from police-union leaders. His remarks when Mulligan introduced the system were recalled and reprinted by newspapers: "It's not fair to the police and it is far too dangerous, as well as an encouragement to all the hoodlums in the country." The alderman had been ill for some time and died the day after Sinclair's slaying.

Within hours of hearing of the murder, the owner of a café near the police station, where Sinclair had often dropped in for coffee, kicked off a spontaneous collection for the family with his own twenty-dollar bill. Money started rolling in. For the time being, the discontent, suspicions, and contemptuous insults that the public had thrown at Vancouver's finest ever since the Tupper Inquiry disappeared. The cold-blooded slaying of a cop touched the city.

The *Vancouver Sun* announced in its first edition that it was setting up a fund for the Sinclairs, kicking it off with a $1, 000 donation. The *Province* announced it would assist with a drive but didn't put up any money. The police union and the department's benevolent association handled all the donations. Generosity was boosted when people learned exactly what benefits were due to the widow and orphans of a slain policeman. It wasn't much. Mrs. Sinclair would get between $50 and $60 a month from her husband's pension fund, and the B.C. Workmen's Compensation Fund would provide $75 a month plus $25 for each child until they reached sixteen years of age. A police mutual-benefit scheme would also contribute a lump-sum payment of about $5,000. The city hadn't had to deal with the consequences of a police killing since 1947.

Money wasn't, however, uppermost in the thoughts of the Sinclair family at their home where they gathered with relatives and friends who arrived in a steady stream to try to comfort them. For seventeen-year-old Ian, now the man of the house, the sight of his father's pipes in full view in the living room was too much, and he put them away upstairs. They had been one of his father's great treasures and were about 150 years old, silver-mounted with Gaelic inscriptions. His mother was too distraught to participate, so Ian took on the responsibility of handling the many things that had to be done following his father's death. First among them was going to the Section Four station on West Boulevard to pick up the family car. He then proceeded with arrangements for his father's funeral. It was to be the type of farewell that always marks the death of an officer on duty.

HEARING ON BANK HOLDUP

YOU BREAK LAWS REGARDLESS OF PERSONAL SACRIFICE AND LOSS.

—*Excerpt from Joe Gordon's final message*

Joe Gordon got a break of sorts, a respite from the intensive questioning he had undergone throughout the night, when he was taken to court on December 8, the morning following his arrest. It was a scheduled appearance regarding the bank-holdup charge in which he had been released on $15,000 bail. Following his sleepless night and despite his obvious fatigue, there was tight security as he entered the court. As he sat down, Gordon gave a weary sigh that could be heard throughout the courtroom. He slumped in his seat, obviously exhausted, his eyes closed. He seemed almost asleep. Gordon was wearing prison clothes and slippers and had a noticeable red welt on his left cheek. The nineteen-year-old woman and the youth arrested with Gordon the preceding night were also in court.

Gordon's lawyer was a man who made his money defending crooks, and he knew all the loopholes in the law. He was described by some as a hard drinker who couldn't make the grade with an established legal firm. Perhaps that is why Larry Hill hustled business at the police station, where he knew the clientele and could usually identify those who might have the money to pay him. He was an astute lawyer, and in this instance he argued on Gordon's behalf that the bank-holdup charge was not properly framed and should be thrown out. "The only link there might be concerning the accused is as an aider and abettor. There is not sufficient evidence to put him on his defence," Hill contended. Magistrate Gordon Scott agreed that the evidence was only circumstantial but said it was enough to remand Joe Gordon for trial. Prosecutor Stewart McMorran immediately linked Gordon to the Sinclair murder. He told the magistrate, "Last night there was a policeman killed by someone, and Gordon is under police surveillance in regard to this matter." McMorran said if bail was to be considered it should be "extremely high." Magistrate Scott remanded the trio until Monday for consideration.

In his younger years, as city prosecutor, Stewart McMorran was involved in many of Vancouver's high-profile cases. In later years, he became a judge. He died in 1998.

Chief Rossiter met with reporters to tell them that the four arrested with Gordon the preceding night had been released from jail. Feeling the heat from the public, which was demanding quick, positive action, he pleaded for assistance from anyone and everyone: "We need all the help we can get." Joe Gordon wasn't talking, and nothing had been shaken loose in the underworld.

The department was for once saved further embarrassment at this trying time when Magistrate Gordon Scott found a beat cop not guilty of trying to extort a couple of bottles of liquor from a taxi driver who had been stopped for speeding.

Mayor Hume revealed that a senior RCMP officer had been offered the job of police chief; it was hoped there would be an announcement about it in a few days. The public perception that a new chief was needed—and the sooner the better—was heightened when the story broke that there was confusion about when a constable was allowed to fire his gun. It resulted from a statement issued earlier in the year after a shot fired at a fleeing car was deemed unnecessary in the circumstances, a relatively minor offence. Some officers took the directive to mean they could only fire if they were shot at first. Brookes, the first patrolman at the scene to see Sinclair in the gutter, commented boldly that in his career he had fired his gun several times and the police brass hadn't appreciated it, although he felt quite justified in each instance. He said he and Wiebe didn't have their guns drawn and certainly didn't know they were chasing cop killers at the Watkins Winram plant when they first arrived.

Rossiter hurried to try to clarify gun policy. He said the earlier statement had made it clear that officers could use their guns if they felt "in danger" or in a dangerous situation. The acting chief explained, "There is no desire that officers should believe that they be restricted to use of arms only in extremity." He added that the law was clear and empowered them to shoot in self-defence. Rossiter added, "They are expected to be prepared at all times to have to resort to use of the gun in defence of themselves in dangerous situations." Alderman Anna Sprott had her own overly simple ideas of what should be done, stating that the police should be able to fire at anyone holding a gun, although "they needn't aim at a vital organ." She confused the quiet deliberation of a shooting range with the drama of split-second action between desperate gunmen and police in dark alleys.

The sad state of the department and the efficiency of the force were brought into sharp focus the next day, December 9, at a police-commission meeting chaired by Mayor Hume. Recruitment and training, or the lack of it, sparked the outburst. It became abundantly clear that the situation wasn't any better in Sinclair's time than it had been in pioneer days. The statement of one retired inspector was repeated, along with the suggestion that the situation now was as it had always been: The inspector had said that on his first day as a patrolman, he found himself on the street with a gun just 24 hours after he was hired. He had had no training and had never before held a gun in his hand.

Magistrate Orr had suddenly resigned as a police commissioner in November, and although he maintained the Tupper report on the Mulligan Affair had nothing to do with it, it was so soon after the report's release that few believed him. Whether he was ashamed that the commission did not fire Mulligan sooner or if he was simply tired of explaining his role in the inquiry to others, it cannot be known. He was a well-known, popular veteran magistrate, and when he and the members of the commission disagreed about a recommendation that a fourth member be appointed, he may have used his objections to a fourth commissioner to cover the fact that he simply had had enough.

The provincial government had rejected Hume's choice of a city prosecutor to replace Orr, preferring some fresh outside blood, and appointed a war hero and city lawyer, 50-year-old Brigadier William Murphy, CBE, DSO. The fourth new member was still to be named. Murphy, a gung-ho type with a brisk military manner, marked his first commission meeting by launching a bitter attack on the city's overall management of the police department and in particular, its lack of proper training.

Murphy grabbed headlines with his angry assertion that Sinclair had never had a day's training in the fourteen years he was a policeman and that this lack might have cost him his life. Rossiter confirmed that training had not been given to the slain policeman or many other veteran members of the force. The brigadier, who had 35 years army service in peace and war, said he was shocked and appalled to find that the department's total training budget for the year was a paltry $500, less than a dollar per cop. A concerned Hume, a man who in a later age might have been dubbed "Teflon Fred" because he was a past master at extracting himself from the glue and sharing it around, was intensely keen on maintaining his image as a competent civic leader. He hurried to explain that $500 was all the training money the departed Mulligan had requested, but Murphy wasn't mollified. Again, the commission had apparently simply accepted the chief's recommendation without question.

Murphy said a survey he had carried out on the 662 personnel in the department revealed that 24 percent had no training at all. He also found that only 4 percent had any kind of advanced, specialized training, and it was possible for a policeman to write promotion examinations without having had any training at all. He called on city council to provide money for a training centre "so that no more lives may be lost needlessly." Hume looked most unhappy as Murphy stressed, "I think it is a scandal that the city police force has been treated in the way it has in respect to training. We must get the money from council to ensure proper training. It is false economy to allow this situation to go on as it has; we must have the money." The mayor hurried to say he would take up the issue immediately.

The new commissioner wasn't through. He claimed that the public perception of a Vancouver policeman was "a fat man with a billy stick." He didn't blame the force, adding, "It has been astonishing to me that this police force has been able to do the job it has done." Murphy re-emphasized that the men badly needed support and he was determined to ensure it was forthcoming. If the department needed money, the city would have to shake the coffers and provide it. While the public and officials wanted security, spending on the police department was often well down on the taxpayers' list of priorities. The brigadier contended that Vancouver could have a first-rate department within three years if it would spend the money. He sarcastically criticized officials who held the purse strings, commenting that this could be done at the expense of getting along "with a few less rose bushes in Stanley Park." Taking Vancouver's love of parks into consideration, this was a bold statement. The commissioner added that there were excellent training facilities elsewhere in Canada and the United States where police could be trained until Vancouver had its own centre. The commission also ordered a complete review of the one-man car policy.

At the next meeting the chastised city council ordered an immediate start on training facilities and put up a $5,000 reward for Sinclair's murderer in addition to the $1,000 already posted personally by Mayor Hume.

The *Sun* continued its harangue that the city was "near a complete breakdown in law enforcement," making hay of Murphy's revelations. *Sun* columnist Jack Wasserman had joked earlier that the

Mayor Fred Hume (left) announces the appointment of George Archer as chief of the Vancouver Police Department, replacing the disgraced Walter Mulligan.

police budget badly needed balancing and that a fund was needed to help. Surprisingly, several people took his column seriously and sent in a few dollars. Wasserman said the $20 he had received would go to the Sinclair fund.

Word soon circulated in the ranks that the new chief would be veteran RCMP Superintendent George Archer, head of the B.C. detachment, a no-nonsense, ramrod-straight disciplinarian regarded as a committed and efficient policeman. Initial public and media reaction to this news was good.

The department had to cope with other problems, including a sudden rise in downtown gatherings of rowdy youths fuelled by heavy beer drinking, which often wound up with fighting and violence. One night a mob of about a hundred congregated at Robson and Seymour, and there were injuries and arrests. When a reporter asked frazzled Superintendent Jack Horton how many men he had on the youth detail, the usually cooperative Horton barked back, "None of your business." Rossiter, who had asked the press for all its support in finding Sinclair's killer, rushed in to fix another hole in the department's public image.

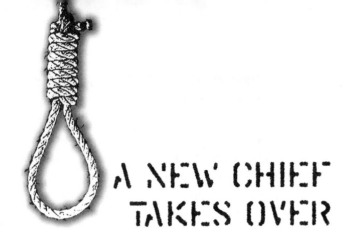

A NEW CHIEF TAKES OVER

YOU BECOME BRUTAL AT TIMES, BITTER ALWAYS.

—Excerpt from Joe Gordon's final message

City police working on the Sinclair investigation were getting desperate. They couldn't hold Gordon much longer if they didn't lay a charge, and Gordon remained close-mouthed, revealing nothing. They had pumped everyone in the underworld with any connection to Gordon, so far without results. Every detective who could be spared from regular duty was working on the investigation. The heat on skid row was intense. Even the reward money had failed to bring forward any information. It was appreciated along skid row that squealing on the popular Joe Gordon could be a very dangerous, even a deadly, thing to do.

One reporter asked Inspector Horton how long the police could hold Gordon without laying a charge. He replied, "On the evidence we have we can hold him as long as we have to." Horton, however, was on shaky ground. There wasn't enough evidence for a charge, and the police couldn't hold Gordon indefinitely on suspicion alone. The papers noted that the police normally could not hold a suspect much more than 24 hours in such circumstances, although there were exceptions.

Fury and frustration mounted in the force on Monday, December 12, when Magistrate Scott again set bail at $15,000 on the October bank-holdup charge. Gordon's lawyer paid it, and the men on the case again watched, enraged, as their chief suspect, the man they were sure was guilty of murder, went free and walked cockily out of the station to a boisterous welcome from his friends.

In a short hearing on December 12, coroner Glen McDonald and a six-man inquest jury heard Dr. T.R. Harmon testify that Sinclair died "almost instantly." One bullet had ripped through his cheek and into his brain; the shot to his face was fired from about two feet away. The other slug went into his back, near the spine, but in all likelihood he was dead before it struck him.

Police-union president Fred Dougherty immediately raised the one-man car issue and bitterly attacked the missing Mulligan. He charged that the ex-chief had introduced the scheme in September 1954 as a squeeze play after council turned down his bid for 50 new recruits. The lack of funds wasn't all Mulligan's fault, but Dougherty damned the policy as "political" without regard for the dangers it presented in everyday policing. The union leader contended bitterly that Mulligan had acted on theory and, to his knowledge, "never operated a patrol car in his life." Dougherty stated that only one other city of comparable size in Canada had one-man cars, and only one in 25 American cities of the same size operated under that system.

Constable Brookes told the inquest that he would have done the same as Sinclair had upon arriving to answer the call of prowlers near the fuel depot, leaving his gun in its holster as he got out of the car. Repeating earlier comments he had made on the apparent confusion in the department about the use of guns, he testified, "I have used my gun several times while on duty and they (the senior officers) didn't appreciate it."

The Nielsens repeated their story of their seeing two men acting suspiciously that night and calling police. Gordon Goll, the first area resident at the scene, testified that he saw the cruiser and Sinclair lying beside it, and a man and woman sitting in a convertible parked nearby. There was a certain irony in the fact that when Goll left his apartment he was carrying a hunting rifle that he put in his car to return to a friend. There were comments as to what might have happened if the two men at the plant, or those still in the car, had seen a man with a rifle walking toward them. Gun-toting Goll appeared to have been very lucky on that night to avoid what was at least one very itchy trigger finger.

The inquest was over quickly, the jury finding that Sinclair had been murdered. It also sided with union leader Dougherty on the question of patrol-car policy. The jury foreman read the verdict: "We are of the opinion that one-man patrol cars do not serve the purpose of law and order."

While his father's death was being probed, young Ian Sinclair and the police were making arrangements for the officer's funeral. His mother was too distraught to make suggestions for a service that would recognize the sacrifice of her fallen husband. The service was to include an honour guard and the band that Sinclair had led piping Scottish tunes. In addition, extensive preparations were needed to accommodate the hundreds of colleagues who would march to the service in order to pay tribute to one of their own.

Some of Sinclair's closest friends were members of the Vancouver Police Pipe Band. Pictured are (left to right): Constable Gordon Sinclair, Detective Sergeant Donald MacDonald, Constable Bert Dawkins, Detective John McHardy, and Detective Duncan Ferguson. Donald MacDonald played the pipes at Sinclair's funeral.

Unlike the day on which Sinclair died, Tuesday, December 13 dawned clear, crisp, and sunny. The 1,500 seats in St. Andrew's-Wesley United Church at Nelson and Burrard Streets were filled long before the service began. It was attended by a great cross section of Vancouver people, ranging from civic officials to ordinary citizens. It included more than 400 Vancouver City policemen, along with representatives from other Lower Mainland departments, scarlet-coated Mounties, and officers from cities in Washington and Oregon. Local firemen from various municipalities were also present in uniform. Hundreds had filed past the casket as it lay in state in the church before the service began. It was flanked by four of Sinclair's colleagues.

The Reverend F.G. St. Denis was the rector of the city's Mount Pleasant Presbyterian Church and the minister who had married the Sinclairs in Trail in 1938. He spoke emotionally of a man he knew well. St. Denis said Sinclair had faced danger many times during his long police career, but on the night of December 7, "with no attempt at heroism he died a hero in the most simple and profound meaning of the word."

St. Andrew's-Wesley's minister, Reverend C.R. Cunningham, prayed that Sinclair's death "will lead to a renewed effort to stamp out crime which has plagued this city constantly in the last year." Many in the large audience whispered a fervent amen to this.

The congregation sang the 23rd Psalm. The service was quietly emotional but not long. Mourners filed out to join the crowd of people outside who had been unable to get into the church. They watched as six policemen carried out the flag-draped coffin bearing Sinclair's cap. The sound of a lament echoed through the normally busy but now closed and silent street as Detective Don MacDonald played the pipes.

In keeping with a Scottish pipers' custom, Sinclair's beloved ancient pipes were draped in black and carried in reverse at the head of the long parade that moved slowly down Burrard to Georgia and then east to Richards. The hearse was flanked by policemen and preceded by the department's pipe band, which had so recently included the man in the coffin. Also marching were the Seaforth Cadet Band, in which Ian Sinclair played, the Vancouver Firefighters'

Crowds lined Burrard Street for the funeral of Gordon Sinclair, which was attended by policemen from Washington State and Oregon, as well as many members from Canadian police forces. The Seaforth Cadet Band, the Vancouver Firefighters' Band, and the Powell River Pipe Band participated in the parade.

Band, and the Powell River Pipe Band, which Sinclair had trained. The parade ended at Georgia and Richards, and a funeral cortege drove to Sinclair's final resting place at Forest Lawn Cemetery.

That night as they read the newspaper accounts of the funeral, Vancouverites were reminded again of the dangers that police work entailed. A short story from Toronto, Ontario, reported that Constable John Earles, after chasing and cornering a car thief, watched the man suddenly whip out a sawed-off shotgun and fire it into his face. The shot tore out one of his eyes, but miraculously the constable survived. Vancouver residents were also touched by a story about Vancouver schoolchildren collecting their pennies to give to the Sinclair fund.

Within days the Sinclair fund had surpassed $5,000, including $500 raised by the B.C. Pipers' Association for its former president. It was to top at about $15,000 and proved to be a godsend for the young widow now raising three children alone.

The day after the Gordon Sinclair funeral, Rossiter announced that two-man patrol cars were operating downtown and, in an effort to combat the escalating late-night crime, another shift had been introduced that would work from late evening until early morning. The acting chief added that the department would be further aided by the arrival from the manufacturer of new high-speed Meteor squad cars.

Twenty-four hours later it was confirmed officially that RCMP Superintendent George Archer would be the new police chief. RCMP Commissioner L.H. Nicholson, in Ottawa, had given permission for the soon-to-retire Archer, aged 58, to leave early in order to assume his new role. Archer had headed the RCMP in Vancouver since 1950. English-born, he had served in Greece and Turkey during the First World War, becoming a sergeant. He moved to Canada after the war, worked in security, and then joined the RCMP. Archer was going to cost the taxpayers a lot more than had Mulligan, but nobody was complaining. Obviously, the city had to pay well to get a replacement acceptable to the force and to the public. Mulligan had received an underpaid $10,000, boosted by what he obtained in graft. Archer would receive $12,000 annually plus another $8,000 a year for reorganizing the force.

It seemed an odd way to ensure him $20,000, twice Mulligan's salary, but the cost didn't bother the public or the media, who hailed the arrival of an experienced veteran whom they hoped would revitalize a demoralized department and herald a new era in a city that badly needed good policing. Archer was to show his worth, eventually being acclaimed as possibly the best chief ever. He was a tall, trim, stern-looking man who didn't suffer fools gladly, but he had a warm side to him and a willingness to praise and reward his men for a job well done. Even with his militaristic insistence on neatly pressed uniforms, well-polished boots, and short haircuts, he proved popular. Along with the spit and polish, Archer was a modern leader eager to innovate, inspire, and develop. He hadn't come from within the Vancouver force, but no senior officers complained—a sign that he was admired for his past performance.

As Archer prepared to take over the department, he knew he could depend on the courts to mete out tough justice with heavy fines and often extremely stiff sentences. On December 19, Mr. Justice J.V. Clyne landed like a ton of bricks on five men convicted of attempted murder and breaking a victim's legs in the drug wars. Clyne, a stern-faced man who looked as tough as the sentences he dispensed, gave them each twenty years in prison. The convicted men were long-time criminals, recently arrived from Montreal: Robert Tremblay, 33; Marcel Frenette, 28; Charles Talbot, 36; Lucien Mayers, 48; and James Malgren, 36. They blanched, and some members of their families in the crowded courtroom cried out as Clyne handed down the penalties. At the sentencing, Clyne told the accused that the people of Vancouver were "heartily sick" of the mounting gang warfare. He turned back on them one remark made by defence lawyers during the trial. In trying to denounce Kinna, the victim, who gave his evidence from a wheelchair, the lawyer had contended "nothing is too bad for a man engaged in the drug business." Clyne noted that Frenette was the only one of the five without a record, but he was in the drug business and he got twenty years because he swung the iron bar that smashed Kinna's legs. The public soon read about him again when he was involved in a hostage-taking of guards at the B.C. Penitentiary. Mayers served only thirteen years of his sentence, but he was safer there than on the streets of Vancouver, where he was found murdered about a year after his release. Informants told police that some members of the underworld believed he was a police stool pigeon. His murder was not solved until there was a review of the case in 2001. Forty-five years after the gang attack on Kinna, a contract killer named Smith was charged with Mayers' murder.

The crime statistics for the previous twelve months were an indication of the job facing Chief Archer. They showed a 10 percent increase, with a sharp hike in the number of serious offences, adding up to over a staggering 14,000. There had been nine murders, two more than in the previous year.

Solid evidence against Gordon continued to elude police; their non-stop investigation failed to come up with anything that would put him back behind bars. Always anxious to taunt the police if he could, and as cocky as ever, Gordon showed up one day at the police station to reclaim a blue overcoat that had been seized when the police apprehended him and his friends in the Burrard Street apartment. The police, ever leery that he might skip town and head for eastern Canada or flee to the United States, continued to dog his every move as he cruised skid row with his friends. The sad segment of society there continued to see Gordon as a heroic figure.

Early on December 23, Gordon was suddenly back in custody. Many wondered about the odd event that put him there. Did it happen as the police said, or did the incident actually happen at all? Joe Gordon was unpredictable, but he knew he was under surveillance. Under the circumstances, would he carry a gun, and would he bother with the small take from a taxi driver whom he allegedly threatened in Stanley Park? It seems unlikely he would risk arrest for so small an amount and then let the cabbie go so the police could be called. Nonetheless, Gordon was apprehended, whisked off to jail and charged with possession of an offensive weapon.

There was speculation among reporters that the incident might have been a set-up, organized by frustrated men in the department and generated by their hatred of and inability to corner the man they were sure had murdered Sinclair. Emotions ran deep and anything was possible in these unruly years. Mulligan had fled Vancouver, but the police force he left behind reflected the chaos that had developed during his final years as chief.

Putting Joe Gordon behind bars was a major development in the case, and now that any chance of flight was cut off, the police investigation began to move more quickly. The Stanley Park offensive weapon incident, the attempted holdup, or whatever it was, quickly disappeared from the docket. Nobody really looked into the bizarre events of that day. Perhaps Mulligan's system of ignoring certain offences was still in effect. Several reporters wondered about it but didn't pursue the matter. It was never fully aired in court, and all record of this arrest of Joe Gordon has since vanished.

When Gordon appeared in court later the same day he was picked up, the *Sun* said he sat in the dock, wearing a black and green shirt under a grey overcoat, not his usual dapper self. He was impassive and didn't look at anyone. Again, Larry Hill represented him. Gordon's appearance in court was over in a matter of minutes; Magistrate Gordon Robson remanded him in custody. The incident was reported in a very short, front-page story in the *Sun* without any reference to the Sinclair slaying; nevertheless, reporters and readers alike knew who Gordon was and also knew the significance of his arrest. Surprisingly, the remand appearance was not even mentioned in the home edition of the *Province*.

What really happened, or didn't happen, will never be known. A request to the police department for the actual wording of the arrest warrant reported in police books at the time produced nothing, only the comment that the files are retained for only seven years and are no longer in existence.[2] With no way of knowing who the arresting officers were that night in Stanley Park, and nobody left to comment who was directly involved in the Joe Gordon affair, the incident remains an unanswered question.

The biggest development in the Sinclair case since the gunshots of December 7 came in the early hours of the final day of 1955. After more than three weeks of investigating, detectives were finally convinced they had enough evidence to charge Joe Gordon with the murder of Gordon Sinclair. The accused was driven that same day from Burnaby's Oakalla Prison to Vancouver.

In the courtroom, Gordon once again showed no emotion in a brief appearance when the charge was formally read, and he was remanded in custody. Oakalla was a particularly porous prison, so a very tight watch was clamped on Joe Gordon. The authorities were taking no chances that he might escape.

Police detectives were elated. Even frequently brusque Superintendent Horton was chatty with reporters when it was announced that there was a big break in the case. Crown prosecutor Stewart McMorran went further, saying that events "moved very quickly yesterday afternoon." Whatever the undisclosed events were, they were not directly linked to anything Gordon did or said because he was already in jail. The public wondered what had happened, especially when one senior officer stated confidently, "We have broken the case and we have all the particulars." The bold statement seemed contrary to the premise that an accused is innocent until proven guilty, but this was a cop killing, and Gordon was the man they had wanted. For Gordon, it was not a happy New Year, and his prospects for 1956 looked grim.

PRELIMINARY HEARING

PRISON TAUGHT ME WHAT I KNOW AND IS TEACHING OTHERS.
THE ONLY FRIENDS IN LIFE I HAVE ARE CRIMINALS. DUE
PROCESS OF LAW BROUGHT ME INTO CONTACT WITH THEM IN
THE FIRST INSTANCE.

—*Excerpt from Joe Gordon's final message*

Charging Gordon with murder was one thing; proving it was another, despite the police contention that they had their man and it was all over except for the formalities. There would be a trial if he pleaded not guilty, and there was little doubt he would do so, as confessing was not in his nature. First came the preliminary hearing, however, to establish whether or not there was sufficient evidence to put him on trial for Sinclair's slaying. It was set for January 12, 1956.

Police legwork now began to pay off. On January 3 police issued an all-Canada warrant for the arrest of Donald Harold Carey, alias Edward Karie and known as "Jimmy" along skid row. A relative newcomer to Vancouver, he was a 26-year-old with a criminal record for minor offences but nothing involving violence. Carey had recently begun to frequent the Hastings strip, and he soon became a consort of crooks and a friend of Gordon's. He was slightly built, about 5 feet 9 inches tall, good-looking, and adorned with numerous body tattoos. His appearance, his dress, and his attitude in many ways resembled those of Gordon, and they were known to have been close acquaintances in the weeks before Sinclair's killing. Police detectives dug up the fact that Carey had left town immediately after the Sinclair shooting and was probably headed for Toronto, his home town. Police became convinced he was the second man seen at the Watkins Winram plant.

The arrest warrant for Carey was one more piece in the puzzle as the public waited for the evidence to unfold in what was expected to be a sensational case based on the facts already known and the rumours that were spreading of dramatic developments. There had been some intriguing testimony from the inquest on December 12, but that had only been a taste, a sample of what was to come. Eyewitness statements from some of the people at the scene indicated there had been at least four people involved. They had told the coroner's jury that two men got out of a car; their furtive manner aroused suspicions as they approached the fuel-company plant. One witness had also seen a man and a woman in a car parked in the nearby alley, and these two were now identified as Noreen Carey and Bob Smith. Also divulged at the inquest were the movements of the escape car that was cut off by Constable Wiebe. Two men had jumped out and fled before the vehicle took off again and became lost in traffic. Later, the car was found abandoned.

The search for Carey went on in Vancouver and in eastern Canada while local ministers and ardent church members debated the evils of allowing professional sports to be played on Sunday afternoons, which they were sure would further the cause of crime and create another breach of the Christian lifestyle. From some fiery preachers in church pulpits came the cry that allowing sports on Sunday would put the city farther along the path to sin and degradation. A city referendum narrowly approved the playing of games on Sunday afternoons by a vote of 38,210 to 36,535. At issue was the schedule for the minor league baseball club. The dire warnings from the pulpit had cagey Premier W.A.C. Bennett stalling. The provincial government controlled the city charter, and he was refusing the required permission from Victoria because he was well aware of the voting support he received from fundamentalist religious groups in Vancouver and in the Bible Belt of the B.C. Interior. After much hassling and delay, Vancouver finally heard the cry "Play ball!" and civilization locally continued as it had before.

Finally it was January 12 and Gordon's preliminary hearing opened to a packed house. Some spectators had shown up in the darkness of early morning before the doors opened in order to be sure of getting a seat. There remained a considerable lineup still waiting for any seat that might become vacant. Sensational evidence arrived as expected and soon had the whole town talking. It came from Noreen Carey, and it startled even seasoned crime watchers who thought they had heard everything.

Noreen Carey was a tall, dark, attractive, slightly plump woman in her late twenties, definitely headline-making material even without the evidence she gave. As the common-law wife of the hunted Jimmy Carey, she quickly established that she was an also-ran in any Mother of the Year contest when she calmly admitted to prosecutor Stewart McMorran that she was the woman who was seen in the car at Watkins Winram. There were gasps of disbelief in the courtroom as amazed onlookers heard her explain matter-of-factly that she had taken her six-week-old baby, Lesley, along for the ride to the fateful robbery attempt under the Granville Street Bridge ramp.

When she revealed she was Carey's common-law wife, she was asked to write her real married name on a piece of paper. She passed it to Magistrate Gordon Scott, who read it but did not speak the name aloud. Throughout the Gordon trial she was always referred to as Mrs. Carey. In a low voice that at times was hard to hear, she told a confusing story of what appeared to be an unplanned, unpredictable, disorganized late afternoon and evening on December 7. She said Gordon came to their east-end apartment about 5:30 p.m. and brought at least one gun into the house with him. He and Carey talked for a bit and then Carey said they were all going out in the car. Gordon picked up the gun as they left. At 52nd and Victoria, the three of them met Bob Smith, a burly 6-foot 4-inch man, who was parked in another car at the side of the road. Gordon pulled in behind him, and Smith immediately got out and jumped into Gordon's car.

As they headed downtown, Noreen told the preliminary hearing, Gordon explained that he had to have $500 by 2:30 p.m. the next day because he was scheduled to appear again in court on the bank-holdup charge and, as he put it, "the fix was in." Questioned by McMorran about this statement, she said Gordon claimed that if he had $2,000 he wouldn't have to stand trial, and he needed $500 immediately to secure the deal. The scenario sounded far-fetched and implausible, but just may have been possible in view of recent revelations from the police department. Many wondered if Gordon actually could have beaten the charge by placing money in the hands of the right person.

Noreen said Joe and Jimmy got out of the car when they got to the Watkins Winram plant and walked to the back of the building. She stayed in the car with Smith and the baby; they parked in the lane behind the building and turned off the engine. Only moments later, they heard the shots. Noreen never thought it was a car backfiring. The two men raced back to the car and jumped in; Smith slammed the accelerator to the floor and they screamed off, burning rubber, with Constable Wiebe in hot pursuit. As the spectators listened in disbelief Noreen recalled, "I was holding the baby and giving her the bottle and I said, 'Don't go so fast. There is a police car behind us.'" She said Joe Gordon had excitedly cried several times that he wanted out, repeating, "I shot the guy." There was a sudden hush in the room as spectators realized that if these *were* his words, they would condemn Joe Gordon to the gallows. He sat quietly in the prisoner's box, his face pale, but he gave no hint of his feelings or apprehensions. Nobody knew better than he the significance of the words he had spoken only seconds after the gunfire at Watkins Winram, where a cop lay dead.

It was only necessary at this hearing for the prosecution to present sufficient evidence to have the accused committed for trial. Noreen would give more intriguing testimony at a later date and would then face searching cross-examination from Gordon's defence lawyer. On the basis of what she had already revealed, many in the courtroom wondered why she also wasn't being charged in the affair. Others were convinced she had been offered a deal if she testified.

A man with a long record, Bob Smith took the stand and stated that he first met Gordon while doing time at B.C. Penitentiary. He claimed that when he originally got in Gordon's car, he thought they were simply going for a "pleasure drive." He denied that they had set out on a crime spree. He then repeated Noreen's version of events, but went further, contending that Gordon was more than excited and closer to hysterics after he spotted the pursuing cruiser. He reiterated Noreen's evidence that Gordon admitted to killing a "guy" at the plant. Smith said both Joe and Jimmy jumped out when he slowed down and stopped the car as the pursuing constable pulled alongside in another car. He said Noreen also tried to get out of the car but Jimmy pushed her back in. After backing into the intersection, he said, they roared off again and lost Wiebe in heavy traffic. They abandoned the convertible a few blocks later and jumped aboard a city bus, taking a short ride to the downtown area. The two then took a taxi back to Smith's car. He said he then drove Noreen to a friend's home in Burnaby. With Smith's evidence it became clear that these two were to be key witnesses for the prosecution and would avoid any charges themselves.

Inspector Pete Lamont testified he was the lead investigator. Prominent in the hunt since the beginning, he was one of the city's biggest, toughest cops. He was a veteran who knew Vancouver's skid-row environment as well as anyone on the force, if not maybe too well: He had long been a familiar figure to crooks. The evidence presented during the Mulligan inquiry had drawn media attention and cast a suspicious shadow over his integrity. Although only the ex-chief and his accomplice, Sergeant Cuthbert, had been cited directly in Tupper's 75,000-word report as being on the take, Lamont had not emerged from the hearings unscathed. Constable Lorne Tompkins had told the inquiry that he saw the inspector receive a large amount of money in a bookie joint.

Lamont told Gordon's preliminary hearing that other detectives working under him were Laurie McCullough, Bill Scott, Al Steen, Joe Cotter, and Roy Tabbutt. Without saying what tip-off led them to an apartment block at 1350 Burrard Street, about eight blocks from the plant, Lamont said Gordon and the others were taken into custody about three hours after the killing. No one in the suite offered any resistance, and, Lamont said, Gordon was sitting beside a phone when they entered. The inspector said he seized a brown-paper parcel that

Gordon admitted was his. It contained a pair of brown shoes and a pair of pants, both splattered with mud. The detective said he also noted that Gordon had a large, fresh scratch on his face.

Presenting new evidence, Lamont had the packed courtroom hanging on every word. They were totally intrigued when he said that a man named James Miller had taken him to the rear of the Fairview Gospel Hall at 1666 West Tenth on December 18, 1955. Under an old tree stump covered by bramble bushes, they dug down and recovered a dirt-coated .38 Webley revolver. The gun was presented as an exhibit and as the likely murder weapon. Every eye in the courtroom was drawn to it.

Forensic expert Detective Sergeant Percy Easler took the stand and confirmed that the gun that had fired the deadly bullets was a long-barrelled .38. He looked at it closely and said it bore the serial number 46339. He said it was an old army weapon but had never been reported stolen or missing, and he had not so far been able to trace its history; however, he was sure "it was the gun that killed Sinclair." It held two empty shells and four live ones when recovered. Ballistics tests showed that the two bullets that killed Sinclair had been shot from its barrel. Gordon looked at the gun as he sat in the box, but his blank expression didn't change.

Gordon had shown no emotion when Noreen Carey and Bob Smith testified, obviously knowing they had made a deal to testify for the Crown. He also remained impassive as Miller testified, knowing he was a stoolie who had also cut a deal, either for money—$6,000 being offered in rewards—or in a bid to have his punishment for a long line of criminal offences reduced. A hardened criminal, Miller had already spent long years in jail for a great variety of offences. Miller was a classic example of the movie stoolie: a shifty, scraggy, snaggle-toothed, 45-year-old with a record as long as your arm—a man who would sell anyone for a buck. It was not hard to be suspicious of everything he said, but as his story tumbled out, it seemed there might be some truth to his words for a change. His testimony would be a major factor in nailing Joe Gordon.

Miller told the hearing very matter-of-factly that he had supplied the murder weapon. Predictably, his involvement with

Gordon had its beginnings in a skid-row beer parlour. He had met the accused in the Anchor Hotel on December 2, at which time Gordon had demanded that Miller get him a gun. It didn't take Miller long to come up with one, and he said he gave the Webley to Gordon that night. Miller was a convicted drug addict and pusher, among many other things, and he said he gave Gordon the gun that night to settle a drug debt.

Asked by McMorran why Gordon had not obtained a weapon himself, Miller replied, "He had too much heat on him." The witness said that about December 16 he asked Gordon for the gun back and was directed to the yard behind the gospel hall on West Tenth. He didn't find it on his first trip and had to go back and ask Gordon for additional directions. Two days later he uncovered the .38. Accompanying him this time, however, was Lamont, who seized the weapon and immediately turned it over to police ballistics experts for testing.

Many of Joe Gordon's friends were among those who filled the front rows for his preliminary hearing, and contempt showed clearly on some faces as they became aware that Miller had made a deal with police that would help nail Gordon. The witness admitted he had been arrested on a drug-possession charge two days before Sinclair's death. It was later disclosed that the deal he had made with detectives, although it was initially denied, was that he would be released from jail at least temporarily in exchange for the information he gave on the stand. Asked why he didn't get in touch with Lamont until December 18, two days after he couldn't find the gun on his own, Miller answered that he had "more important things to do, like shooting dope." Miller said his regular habit was about six caps a day, costing five dollars each. He stated without hesitation that it would be more if he had the money. When it was put to him that he had a habit of using guns himself, Miller responded, almost boastfully, "Oh, yes, I got ten years and three years in jail for using a gun, but," he said with a smile, "it was many years ago." Miller had been lucky in 1953 to wriggle out of a habitual-criminal conviction. This was one of the reasons the police were able to get him to testify. He was readily prepared to talk if it would keep him out of jail and help avoid the "habitual-criminal" charge that still hung over his head and would surely come up again if he were arrested for any serious offence.

Louise McHardy, a teenager from Langley, in B.C.'s Fraser Valley, was listed as the tenant of the Burrard Street apartment where Gordon was arrested. She and Carl Stromson were apparently acquainted with Gordon and his young girlfriend, and the four of them had spent some time together. On the stand, she said she had earlier seen in Gordon's possession a gun that resembled the murder weapon. Carl Stromson, also of Langley, gave similar evidence. Several other minor witnesses were heard before Magistrate Scott, without hesitation, committed Gordon for Supreme Court trial on the capital charge. April was established as a likely time for the trial. Gordon left the court apparently unperturbed, as always.

JIMMY CAREY ARRESTED

THE PRICE YOU PAY CAN NEVER BE REPAID.

—Excerpt from Joe Gordon's final message

The cross-country search for Jimmy Carey continued, centred in the Toronto area, where local police worked on their informants. Carey soon found he could run but he couldn't hide. On February 14, St. Valentine's Day, he got a present from Toronto police: a set of handcuffs. They had received a tip, so it wasn't by chance that they nailed him walking down a city street. They knew exactly where and when to find him on Spadina Avenue. Carey gave up without a struggle, but what police found when they frisked him was indeed incriminating for someone already listed as a suspect in a West Coast murder. He was carrying an unloaded gun and a knife. Jimmy was flown back to Vancouver and held on a charge of possessing firearms. After four days of intensive questioning, police laid a second murder charge. They believed they had enough evidence, so Jimmy Carey joined Joe Gordon as the accused in the shooting death of Gordon Sinclair.

Justice moved swiftly in 1956, and Jimmy's preliminary hearing opened on March 2. In the first edition of that day's *Vancouver Sun*, Noreen Carey posed prettily, smiling with baby Lesley for a large picture that appeared on the front page. Notoriety seemed to appeal to her. She repeated the same confusing story she had related earlier, but there were a few embellishments. Each of them was aimed clearly at helping Jimmy as much as possible and fingering Joe as the real criminal. She said Joe had played Russian roulette with the gun he brought to their apartment on December 7. Noreen said he removed all the bullets but one from his gun and put them on the arm of the chair. Spectators at the hearing were fascinated as she described how Joe spun the chamber, pointed the barrel at his head and pulled the trigger. It clicked, but there was no explosion. The woman said Gordon laughingly explained that when there was only one bullet in the gun, its weight carried the chamber down so the trigger almost always fell on an empty

Jimmy Carey had a string of aliases. Prior to fleeing from Vancouver to Toronto, he lived with his common-law wife, Noreen, and their baby daughter, Lesley, in a basement suite where they frequently entertained Joe Gordon and his friends.

space. Noreen said she was unconvinced of this theory and took the gun away from him, suggesting it would create unnecessary trouble if he shot himself while visiting them. She also admitted that Jimmy had another gun, which he took with him when they left with Joe and the baby in the car.

She repeated her earlier statement about Joe badly needing money for an alleged bribe in the bank case. Noreen also said that while they were driving in the convertible, Jimmy and Smith told Joe that if he intended to "blow a safe" or something like that, they wanted to make sure they all had a good alibi. She explained that Joe, in his usual swaggering style, told them, "It doesn't matter what the police know; it's what they can prove that counts."

The day after the shooting, the young woman said, Jimmy suddenly arrived at the Burnaby home of Mr. and Mrs. Erwin

McEwen. She said Smith had driven her there the previous night and Carey arrived in the morning. She testified, "He sat down beside the baby and cried. He was just sick to think that the baby and I were there in the car while the chase was underway." Her comments, however, did little to temper the fact that she had quite readily and without hesitation stepped into the convertible with her baby in her arms, knowing that at least two other passengers carried guns. She added that on that terribly unhappy morning Jimmy told her that for a moment at the Watkins Winram plant he had thought Gordon was shooting at him. The statement put Carey at the crime scene, but it also put a gun that had been fired in Gordon's hands.

Noreen said that when Jimmy stated he was going to phone detective Bill Morphitt, whom he knew, and tell him everything, she told him not to. She said she and the McEwens insisted he should get out of town; in fact, she said she would leave him if he didn't. They told Carey that the two most relentless members of the squad, Lamont and McCullough, were on the case. They were all especially worried because Lamont was heading the hunt. As a result of their conversation, McEwen rented a car, drove Carey to Chilliwack in the Fraser Valley, gave him $25, and saw him off on an eastbound bus. Noreen said her only communication with Jimmy prior to his arrest in Toronto was a phone call from Fort William, Ontario. Other witnesses were heard, but the outcome soon became evident: Carey was committed for trial with Gordon in Supreme Court. Noreen Carey made all the visits permissible to see Jimmy in the following weeks, but nobody rushed to spend time with Gordon.

For their parts, Gordon and Carey knew their lives were in the balance because the hangman was still busy across Canada in 1956 and would be until July 14, 1976. Opposition to the death penalty was growing across the country, fuelled by protests and the end of capital punishment in other countries, but men and women still faced the gallows at this time in the Dominion of Canada. They would have had fewer fears had they lived in Britain, where in February of 1956 the House of Commons on a free vote ended death by hanging by a narrow 298–262 margin. Most members of the Conservative government headed by Prime Minister Anthony

Eden voted for retention, including Sir Winston Churchill, but the members were split on the emotional issue. The House of Lords initially opposed the decision, but it eventually was passed.

As the public waited for the upcoming trials of Joe Gordon and Jim Carey, they read about the unabated crime wave that continued to plague them. One of the more unusual robberies occurred when a deputy postmaster hiked over the mountains from Britannia Beach on Howe Sound, northeast of Vancouver, with a backpack containing $44,000 he had stolen. At the time there was no highway connection along Howe Sound between Vancouver and Squamish. He later was traced to Toronto, where police recovered half the money.

Although crime continued to capture most of the big headlines in Vancouver, other happenings occasionally broke through to make news. Canada lost to Russia in the 1956 Olympic hockey contest at Cortina, Italy. Perhaps even worse was the loss of the silver medal by a score of 4–1 to an upstart team from the United States. Being "crippled for life" was worth only $40,026 in a court award to a Penticton, B.C., teenager, Glendine Hatfield, who was accidentally shot. The *Vancouver Daily Province* contended there were lots of affordable homes for those earning a hefty $6,000 a year or more, but what was needed was a house priced at $10,000 for those earning less. Vancouver General Hospital was to have a new 500-bed wing, making its capacity of 1,300 second only to Toronto General. Alcohol, street racing, and speed were just beginning to become a problem in Vancouver, with the toll of young lives lost reaching three in 1956.

Mrs. Helen Orsolete, 44, a widowed Austrian immigrant dishwasher in a school cafeteria, won $140,000, a fortune then, in the Irish Sweepstake lottery. William Drew De Geer and his bride of nineteen hours, both from Vancouver, died when their borrowed honeymoon car plunged down a mountainside near Hope, B.C. Contractor John McElroy was lauded when he cancelled a deal to sell his new apartment block in New Westminster, 41 suites costing about $300,000, to American buyers. McElroy struck a blow for race relations and turned down the prospective buyers after they said a local businesswoman, Susan Chew, would not be allowed to move in despite having put down a deposit because they didn't rent to "people of her nationality." In Seattle a gas war toppled prices to 25.8 cents a gallon. Vancouver's nemesis, rain, was blamed for most of the $60,000 loss in 1955 suffered by Stanley Park's outdoor musical company Theatre Under the Stars. A 23-year-old schoolteacher, Pat Nelson, won a $2,600 car in New Westminster at what was dubbed the biggest bingo game ever held in western Canada. The legality of such events under the existing gambling laws was being studied by legal experts, and the police were poised if need be to close them down and lay charges.

Vancouver's Police Commission made news of its own. Unhappy with Tupper's indirect criticism of how they had operated in Mulligan's time, one of its members, Judge Rey Sargent, decided to announce his resignation. On March 15 he was replaced by Colonel Cecil Merritt, a lawyer, member of an old Vancouver family, and a war hero who had won the Victoria Cross for his bravery in the Dieppe debacle in France in the Second World War. His father had been one of the fallen in the First World War. Vancouver sent a lot of men to the front in both world wars and paid a very heavy price. Mayor Hume again had wanted a member of the city's legal staff appointed to the post, but the provincial government, wisely for once, preferred someone well removed from the past, and under the terms of the city charter the province had the final say.

Wanting to make an impression with the force, Merritt declared that the commission had cleared every person in the department. This wasn't actually the case, because Commissioner Tupper had left a lot of questions unanswered. The public still remembered Sergeant Cuthbert's statement that more than half of the gambling squad was on the take, and the collective amnesia that its members had when called to testify, all claiming they were either unaware of what was going on or couldn't remember the claims that had been made about graft and corruption. There still were many reservations about the Vancouver Police Department, but Merritt was advocating a new start. City council had heard Tupper's call for a larger force to meet the needs of a fast-growing city and gave approval for an increased budget. This would give Archer 39 new policemen at an additional cost to taxpayers of $102,000, less than $3,000 a year per new recruit, but with this incentive Archer was well on his way to a complete reorganization of the force.

Very tough sentences continued to be handed down in local courts. "There is no place in society for men who carry guns in the commission of crime," said Mr. Justice H.W. McInnis, sentencing Harold Coullier, 36, to fifteen years in jail for a bank holdup, on top of six years he was serving for another crime. Carl LaVictoire, 36, got twelve years for the same holdup. Mr. Justice McInnis emphasized, "Any such man who appears before this court can expect little consideration."

The police found to their mortification and to the amusement of the public that they had unknowingly been housing a vagrant at headquarters. He was sleeping in an old press room in a building adjacent to the main station and had set up light housekeeping with a hot plate pinched from the maintenance room. When finally caught by a caretaker, he was hauled off, protesting that he was an undercover FBI agent.

The department's reputation was saved slightly when Magistrate Thomas Dohm found three policemen not guilty of assaulting a prisoner being held in the city jail. The magistrate found the accused was drunk and that prosecution witness Constable D.C. Trehearn was "prone to exaggeration." Constable Trehearn's subsequent career was undistinguished.

GUN BATTLE
AT THE BANK

REMEMBER, INDIRECTLY WE TAUGHT OUR CHILDREN TO BE DELINQUENTS BUT FAILED TO TEACH THEM THE MEANING OF THE WORD.

—Excerpt from Joe Gordon's final message

As the days ticked away toward April 9, the latest date set for the murder trial of Joe Gordon and Jimmy Carey, another attempted holdup and gun battle took place that would re-echo during their murder trail, as those involved would be called to appear for the defence at the trial of the two accused. It exploded April 3, during the attempted holdup of a suburban bank. Two bullets had killed Gordon Sinclair, but RCMP Constable Bud Johnstone miraculously survived being hit eight times as fusillades of shots were exchanged by Mounties and heavily armed gunmen during the raid. Johnstone was downed in the exchange but struggled back to his feet, his gun firing. He made it to the door, where he saw one robber lying dead outside and another wounded. One surrendered; a fourth man fled in a van, but he was quickly captured when he crashed the vehicle. The $10,523 taken by the bandits was recovered.

Johnstone was one of three RCMP from the Maillardville detachment in Coquitlam who had raced to the bank where manager J.W.D. Howat had managed to trip the alarm as three masked men burst into the bank, which was empty of customers. As the gunmen were scooping up the money the RCMP arrived. Johnstone, a 26-year-old, eight-year veteran, ran in first. As he rushed to the counter, asking if everything was all right, a man jumped up and fired, downing him. The next several seconds were mayhem as bullets flew in every direction and the wounded Johnstone fired back, hitting the gunman.

Johnstone struggled to his feet and advanced to the door in a hail of lead from the other bandits. One came toward him, and the policeman later recalled, "He kept firing at me as he ran towards me. I could feel the bullets hitting." Johnstone emptied his five-shot revolver, making it to the door before collapsing. Inside, bank manager Howat kept the bank's revolver trained on the wounded gunman, who lay on the floor behind the counter. Outside, Constable Al Beach joined in the battle, emptying his weapon, but he was unable to stop the fourth man fleeing in the stolen van. The vehicle crashed after a short chase, and the robber was caught trying to run away. The bandits had come well armed. In the van were two revolvers, a sawn-off shotgun, and two Thompson submachine guns that could have turned the robbery into a slaughter if they had been brought into play. The dead man outside the bank was Herbert Howerton, 23, of Langley, a Korean War veteran. The three others arrested were William Gary Owen, 21, also of Langley, and two Vancouver men, Howard Foster and William Banks.

Johnstone was rushed to hospital, badly hurt but conscious. His wife, a nurse, and their young daughter were taken to his bedside. Doctors were amazed to find he had been hit eight times but had survived serious injury because none of the bullets hit a vital organ. He would live.

Johnstone's recovery also amazed his colleagues. One Mountie said he was like "Fearless Fosdick," a cartoon character of the era who was an FBI agent and was frequently depicted with bullet holes in his chest. Senior RCMP officers went to his bedside to tell him that Ottawa headquarters had promoted him to corporal, bringing his $345-a-month pay to a whopping $385. They were also posting him to take charge of the two-man detachment at the quiet Vancouver Island seaside town of Qualicum Beach.

The dead bandit's father, Herbert Howerton, told reporters that he didn't blame the Mountie for his son's death because the officer was forced to defend himself, but he blasted the army and the federal government for allowing his son to bring home a Thompson machine gun and a Korean burp gun. It was obvious the authorities were unaware that Howerton had brought the guns back and had them in his possession in Canada. The Korean gun had not been brought to the holdup, and where he obtained the second Thompson—the favourite of G-men in the United States in the 1930s as they battled Al Capone, the Mafia, and other gangs—was never ascertained.

The public learned that Howerton was a native of Wilkie, Saskatchewan, who had come to Langley with his family as a young boy. His father said he quit school in Grade 10, worked at odd jobs, fought in a Golden Gloves boxing tournament as an also-ran, and joined the Princess Patricia's Canadian Light Infantry (PPCLI) during the Korean War. He saw a lot of action during the conflict. On his return, Howerton worked for eight months as a prison guard before parting company with the penal authorities. He did nothing much after that, although his mixing with the underworld had drawn police attention and they wondered what he might be up to. His father said he had become worried when his son told him shortly before the attempted holdup that he was due to face a charge of being drunk. Howerton told his son he had no money to help him pay a fine. "I was worried when he said, 'Don't worry, Dad, I won't do any time in jail.'" The father said his son was a changed man when he came back from Korea, more trigger-tempered than he had been before.

Like Gordon and Carey, Howerton was always a snappy dresser. A friend told reporters, "He always wore kid gloves, a Stetson, and smoked a big cigar." He added that after coming back from Korea in the early 1950s, Howerton was a "ferocious guy" who was always looking for a fight. "He didn't know the meaning of fear," said the friend. The parents of one of the other bandits, William Banks, said they had become worried when their son fell in with rowdies after being unable to hold a steady job. The holdup survivors appeared in court and were remanded without bail.

THE TRIAL BEGINS

THEY RELY ON THE TIME-WORN PHRASE, "SOCIETY MUST BE PROTECTED."

—*Excerpt from Joe Gordon's final message*

Joe Gordon and Jim Carey appeared in court on Monday, April 9. Their trial was held in the impressive old stone courthouse building on Georgia Street near Granville, now the Vancouver Art Gallery. Its atmosphere has always promoted a lot of whispering and subdued conversation. Visitors—even some of the accused—often stand in awe of it. As expected, spectators arrived early to line up for seats, eager to hear firsthand the unfolding details in what obviously would be a sensational trial. The preliminary hearing had been riveting; this would be more so. Everyone wanted to see and hear Noreen Carey and her casual mixture of mothering and crime in the Vancouver underworld. The lucky ones at the head of the lineup got seats, but a lot of disappointed people were left in the hallways and outside on Georgia Street.

All eyes were on the accused as scarlet-coated Mounties led them up the stairs from the holding cells and into the prisoners' box. Many of their old cronies watching knew the experience firsthand. As always, the two men were dapperly dressed. Gordon actually changed clothes three times during the trial. For the opening he wore a charcoal grey suit and Carey wore a lighter grey one. They seemed unfazed as they faced the man known as the "Hanging Judge," Mr. Justice Alexander Manson, a controversial figure believed by many

Vancouver's stately old courthouse was the venue for the trial of Joe Gordon and Jimmy Carey. In those days, a driveway led to the front steps and a green lawn stretched right out to the sidewalk. The building became the home of the Vancouver Art Gallery in 1983.

to be B.C.'s worst judge. In his 26 years on the bench, the former politician had more of his rulings changed and altered on appeal than any other judge in the history of the province. When he retired, Manson said he never "lost a night's sleep" over a murder trial and a sentence of death.

Manson dismissed an application for separate trials for the two accused. A twelve-man jury was chosen quickly, and for fifteen days they heard the tragic story of the murder and the lurid details surrounding it from a colourful parade of characters who walked, strolled, or strutted to the witness box in the courtroom. Some witnesses arrived in handcuffs. Little Lesley's mummy, Noreen Carey, continued to amaze everyone. She was one of the stars of the more than 30 witnesses ranging from police technical experts and controversial investigators to a cross section of the city's seedy citizens—hardened criminals, a paroled murderer, and younger violent offenders serving long sentences. Of the eleven defence witnesses, only one did not have a criminal record.

The jurors listened to police denials, witnesses' implausible explanations, contradictions, lies, and a defence claim that few could have imagined. Every day brought something new and unusual. Newspaper readers and radio listeners avidly followed the life-or-death drama starring Joe Gordon and Jimmy Carey. The public particularly wanted to hear Gordon's account of what happened as he fought to save his neck. Few had any sympathy for a man charged with killing a cop, but still, the slightly built, curly-haired, sometimes bespectacled Gordon captured their imaginations. Outwardly he appeared cool and unruffled, but there was a lot of damning evidence, and spectators wondered how he would try to beat the hangman's noose. To crooks and shysters he had become an icon; he was a man who had lost only to the justice system and was still a swashbuckler in the eyes of his peers.

Prosecutor William Schultz was one of the city's most seasoned lawyers, a veteran of years of wide-ranging experience. Larry Hill represented Gordon, and Carey's defence team comprised lawyers Derek Le Page and Norman Mullins.

The prosecutor built his case in an opening 70-minute address. Many of the facts had already been disclosed during the separate preliminary hearings of the two men, Gordon's being held before Carey's arrest in Toronto. Anticipated were more details of the events that took place on the night of the murder and the disclosures that might emerge from the cross-examination of both prosecution and defence witnesses. Schultz caused a stir in the benches when he said Noreen was the one who made the mask for Gordon before leaving their apartment on December 7. A crude white mask had been found near the scene of the shooting. He added that she would also testify that she heard Gordon say he needed money by the next day for a bribe in connection with his bank-holdup charge and he was prepared to get it by robbery. Recounting the scene at Watkins Winram, Schultz looked intently at the jurors and maintained that

During the trial of Joe Gordon and Jimmy Carey, the judge decided the jury should visit the scene of the crime, as well as a nearby church where the murder weapon had been found. Escorted by the police, a handcuffed Joe Gordon kibitzed with onlookers and members of the press. It was his last day out of jail and on the streets of Vancouver.

Gordon and Carey had a common criminal purpose; he contended that they were prepared to use guns "and therefore were guilty of murder."

Hill caused a stir when he maintained that not only would he try to prove that Gordon was nowhere near the scene of the killing, but that he would also try to prove who actually shot Gordon Sinclair. This assertion caused members of the media and spectators to try to guess who he was talking about. It's safe to say that nobody came up with the name that Hill would eventually raise.

There was no doubt in anyone's mind in the coming days that, despite all their denials, the police had cut more deals than could be made in a 24-hour poker party in their determination to get the goods on Gordon. Investigators and Crown witnesses all maintained it wasn't the case, but the facts spoke otherwise. Even Mr. Justice Manson contended that he had not tailored his decisions to meet the needs of police, but it seemed clear that he had.

The trial's second day, Tuesday, was a welcome break from behind bars for Gordon and Carey, and it gave them the chance to get outside on a warm, sunny, spring day. Mr. Justice Manson decreed that the jurors see the Watkins Winram plant and vicinity. They left in the afternoon: judge, jurors, accused, five red-coated Mounties, court officials, and a gaggle of reporters and photographers. Local residents came out to see what was going on, passers-by wondered at the procession, and passing motorists slowed down to have a look. They were joined by a troupe of excited kids on foot and on bicycles and an equally worked-up contingent of local dogs. The youngsters were fascinated by the handcuffs on the accused. A woman summed it up for reporters: "It looks exciting, but I'm darned if I know what it is all about." Her interest soared and she became wide-eyed when she learned that she was looking at two accused murderers.

The jurors were shown the exact spot where Sinclair's body was found, and they retraced the route of the two men who had been seen fleeing the scene. They walked around the plant, carefully picking their way through the garbage that littered the alleys. Manson directed them to study the entire area and the surrounding buildings. He told them to try to imagine what it could have looked like on a dark, poorly lit, rain-swept December night.

Carey tried to avoid looking at the reporters and photographers who elbowed their way as close as possible to the two accused. Carey talked to his lawyer; Gordon tried to conceal his face but soon realized it was a losing battle. He switched his approach and smiled at the newsmen, sticking his tongue out at *Vancouver Sun* photographer Bill Dennett and quipping, "That fooled you." Once again Joe and Jimmy were the best-dressed, smartest-looking pair in the group; the reporters and photographers looked rumpled.

For the accused, it was a couple of hours of sunshine to savour after weeks behind bars. They knew it could be the last time they would ever experience the outdoors, people, traffic, and the day-to-day life of a busy city. If the murder verdicts went against them, they were done. From the plant, the group moved to where the .38 Webley gun had been recovered, by the Fairview Gospel Hall on West Tenth. A sign outside stated "The Blood of Jesus Christ, His Son, Cleaneth Us from All Sin." The accused couldn't miss seeing it, but what they thought no one knew. The wording was coincidental, however appropriate or inappropriate it might have been.

Jurors peered closely at the stump as thick bramble bushes were pushed aside so they could have a look. There was a moment or two of embarrassment for the police when the visit ended and the van transporting Gordon and Carey wouldn't start, but a friendly oil-truck driver came to the rescue and gave the vehicle a push. It started, and the accused were taken back to their cells. The jurors returned to the Hotel Vancouver, adjacent to the courthouse, where they were sequestered for the trial's duration.

In court next day, Hill complained about the *Sun's* front-page picture of the accused at the scene of the crime during the court-supervised visit the previous day. He said it could impair a defence in which identity played a part. He also objected to the extensive coverage of the visit given by the Canadian Broadcasting Corporation on the previous evening's newscast. Manson said the accused had the right to a fair trial and he warned that the "press should err on the safe side by excluding anything that might be calculated even in a minor degree to jeopardize the trial of accused persons." Manson didn't like the media, although he was far from averse to using them for his own purposes when it suited him. Hill said he wanted to reserve the right to reconsider the material and bring forward a motion, but the judge commented, "It's water under the bridge now, but you can recall it." Hill didn't. The *Sun* pulled the picture after the first edition.

Excitement rose in the benches when RCMP Corporal Ed Carter testified. He was called as a witness for the prosecution and told the court, to nearly everyone's surprise, that Carey was a police informant, a stoolie, somebody the underworld hated with murderous venom. Gordon, who may have been ignorant of this fact earlier, obviously had learned more about Carey since his most recent arrest and confinement, because he remained stoic and impassive. He didn't explode or even look slightly surprised at the revelation that he could have been double-crossed by his supposed friend and cohort. The public benches, however, were astir, excited by this new information that could mean the prosecution had an eyewitness to the whole event. It could bring a guilty verdict for the man in the box whose life depended on what was revealed in court.

Gordon had been around long enough to develop a hatred for squealers, but he didn't show it. Carey, surprisingly, also remained impassive as Carter's testimony set him up for a serious beating, even death, if fellow convicts and friends of Gordon's decided to exact the revenge he now had coming, according to their code. He could never again feel safe anywhere on the street or even behind bars. This was the same kind of criminal code that had forced old drug trafficker "Silent Bill" Semenick to keep his mouth shut and refuse to identify in court the two men who had tried to take him for a ride in Stanley Park. Carey sat in the box close to Gordon, his head down, eyes focussed on the floor, unable to look at his old pal.

Corporal Carter said he still was investigating the gangland slaying of Danny Brent, the trafficker found shot to death on the golf course. He testified that two weeks before Sinclair's murder he had talked to Carey and the accused had passed a gun, a possible murder weapon, to him. Carter said he took it to police headquarters, fired a shot, and passed the bullet and the weapon on to ballistics experts. They indicated it was not the weapon that killed Brent; Carter then returned the gun to Carey.

There was no evidence about how the weapon came into Carey's possession. The policeman said he had known Carey for about a year and was also on good terms with Noreen Carey. It was obvious city police had not been totally ignorant of Carey's activities. The court and the spectators, however, learned nothing about Carey's career as an informant. They were not told how long he had acted as an informant or if the police had paid him. The Crown witness did not mention if the police held something over Carey, and there was no cross-examination to delve into the situation. His defence attorney's performance was to become a controversial issue.

The jurors heard technical evidence from various prosecution witnesses before the first eyewitness, Mrs. Nielsen, took the stand. She was asked to take a long look at the accused, but again, as she had done in the lineup at police headquarters immediately after the shooting, she said she could not identify either man as one of the two she had seen walking toward Watkins Winram on December 7. She repeated that one of the men she had seen was much taller than the other. Even with the poor lighting in the area, Mrs. Nielsen was absolutely sure about this difference in height. Manson ordered Gordon and Carey to get out of the box and stand side by side. It was clear the two were similar in height, Carey taller than Gordon only by about an inch.

On the third day of the trial, the early-show regulars once again filled the front rows and every seat in the courtroom. They all waited impatiently for the return of Noreen Carey. She was not to disappoint them. When she entered court it was evident that she had lost weight since her appearance at the preliminary hearing. Her friends said that worrying about Carey had cost her at least twenty pounds. It was quickly established that she was not married to Carey, although she used the accused man's name. She testified that they had lived together for several years and that baby Lesley was their child. The court learned that her legal husband's name was Lewry and that she also had a seven-year-old son living with her parents in Moose Jaw, Saskatchewan. She had already posed with Lesley for the large front-page picture in that day's *Vancouver Sun*. Noreen wasn't shy of the camera, even if she seemed flustered much of the time in the witness box.

In a low, hurried voice she made her first statement: "My minister says the oath means that what I say would have to be the truth. I have been told so many things to say, I am all mixed up." It seemed she had only recently found religion, or rediscovered it, and Manson tried to calm the harried woman. She testified that she lived with Carey and the baby in a basement suite at 6927 Nanaimo Street. Asked to identify Carey, she looked at him with a broad smile, but he stared back, stony-faced.

Noreen repeated that Gordon had arrived at their apartment and sat in an armchair, playing Russian roulette with a gun he had brought with him. She said there was a duster (an old pair of men's underwear) in the house, and when Carey briefly left the apartment Gordon asked her to cut two holes in it to make it into a mask. Asked by prosecution lawyer Schultz to identify the mask introduced as an exhibit, the woman said she thought it was the same one. Told by Manson to have a good look, the flustered Noreen replied, "It looks much like it. Well, yes, I would say it was." Schultz was finding out quickly that his star witness wasn't easy to pin down, and he was becoming exasperated with her.

She was vague about why she had taken the baby with her when the three of them left the house, but gave listeners another reason to believe she was far from the perfect mother: She said that before they left, Carey mixed the formula for the six-week-old baby's bottle, adding nonchalantly that he, not she, did everything for the infant.

Shultz then inquired about Gordon's statement that he needed $500 by the next day for a bribe in his bank-holdup charge and was prepared to hold up ten drugstores if need be to get it. Her testimony rambled and she spoke so quickly and softly that Manson considered sitting her closer to the frazzled court stenographer, who was having trouble catching what was being said. The jury members leaned forward in their seats, trying to hear her low-voiced mumblings. There were complaints later of mistakes in the transcript, hardly surprising in light of the problems the stenographer had. At Manson's urging, Noreen raised her voice and spoke more slowly, at least temporarily.

Asked by Schultz exactly why they were riding around in Gordon's convertible, Noreen, obviously speaking from experience and previous rides around town, said the accused "was writing down addresses; he liked riding around like that a lot." She wasn't pressed on how many times she had taken similar trips with Gordon, or where they went in the city or at what time of the day or night, but the jury was left to ponder whether or not he was casing establishments for future break-ins. She said they pulled up behind the car of another man parked at the sidewalk. He got out and joined them. He was 6-foot 4-inch Bob Smith. She said Carey and Gordon each had a gun, and the two weapons were passed back and forth in the car. Smith finally put the .45 under the seat. Hill again complained that Noreen's rapid mumbling was hard to follow. Mr. Justice Manson, in what was hardly an appropriate comment during a trial for a murder in which a gun was used, commented, "She is very quick on the trigger at times."

Noreen continued and recalled Gordon stating, "Nobody stops me any more, just Devries [a Vancouver policeman]. They think I have a lot of money now." Gordon was guessing that the police had little doubt he was guilty of the bank holdup and still had some of the money.

Noreen testified that Gordon drove them to the Watkins Winram fuel plant, parked in the back lane, got out, and walked down the alley toward the plant. He wasn't gone long; when he returned to the car, he asked Smith to go with him back to the plant. The jury listened carefully to her softly spoken statement when she recalled Smith saying, "You will have to take all the blame, Joe, because you have the .38 and the other gun is under the seat." Noreen said her Jimmy decided to go with Gordon instead.

Pressed about whether or not Smith got out of the car, she replied, "I seem to think that Bob drove down there and then again I seem to think Bob got out first." This contradicted her earlier statement that Gordon drove from her apartment to the site. Schultz knew there would be confusion as her story went on. From her evidence, it seemed that Smith got out of the car only to change seats and then got back behind the wheel, but the three eyewitnesses had testified that one of the men they saw was much taller than the other. Smith was about eight inches taller than the two accused. Spectators' interest became keener when Noreen Carey stated, "Jack Horton told me if I said Bob Smith got out of the car he would take my baby away from me. My Lord, I hid my baby before I came down here because he has threatened me that if I mention his name and anything about Bob Smith getting out they would get me. He said to me, 'I would hate to see you lose your baby, Noreen.' I am not to mention anything about the deal he made with Bob, or the deal Lamont made with McKenzie [the man also known as Miller, who told the preliminary hearing he got the .38 Webley for Gordon] or anybody." The courtroom was hushed as she spoke, engrossed by her revelations about threats and police interference with the testimony she would give as a key witness.

Manson broke into her evidence to say, "If you are under any fear or threats, if any policeman has told you what to say, disregard any threats. If I am satisfied that threats have taken place I will instruct the police to give you additional protection." This brought one of the few roars of laughter heard during the trial. The judge and even the two accused all had smiles on their faces when Noreen plaintively exclaimed, "They are the ones giving me the trouble!" She explained that Lamont had told her it would be better for Jimmy if she left Smith out of her statements and "we all stuck to the same story." She added that the police also told her "not to dare mention" Gordon's claim that he ultimately needed $2,000 for bribery money to fix the bank-holdup charge.

Noreen's voice was fading again, and Manson asked the court reporter to read back what she had said. The stenographer was still having trouble transcribing the woman's whispered comments for the record, so there were complaints from all sides when he read back the transcript. After some discussion and a few amendments, the lawyers agreed on the court's record.

Noreen repeated that she and Smith were in the car when they heard shots and then "everything seemed to happen very fast. Smith started the motor and said we had to get out of there." She told him to wait for Carey. When asked why only Carey and not Gordon, Noreen replied, "Jimmy was the only one I was really interested in." When both men ran up and jumped in, she again described the bizarre scene as she sat in the fleeing car trying to feed the baby. At one point in the swaying vehicle, she said, she was trying to juggle the baby, a bottle, and a blanket. This was when she saw the police car following and issued a warning. She said Gordon shouted several times that he wanted to get out, that "I shot the guy."

During Noreen's evidence, Schultz made a plea for her to be treated as a hostile witness. This would have been a startling turnaround, as she was one of the two key prosecution witnesses. Such a move would have permitted Schultz to cross-examine some of the more surprising and contradictory statements she had just made. Manson denied the request, but he did order that she be held incommunicado for the time being, seeing and speaking only to a police matron. He ordered her detention partly because of her surprise statements and claims that she had been told what to say and threatened by police if she didn't. Noreen didn't seem upset by the decision. As one excited and intrigued elderly spectator commented when he left the court, "Boy, that one's a real cracker."

There was a loud exchange of words between Manson and Gordon's lawyer, Larry Hill, when he started his cross-examination of Noreen. He quoted from the *Province*, which had reported that Noreen said Schultz had told her "what to say." The judge jumped in, saying he had checked this statement in the transcript and found that she had actually stated the prosecutor told her "… not to say …" In light of her mumbling and the court reporter's problems, it was impossible to know exactly what she actually *had* said. She wasn't asked to clarify this point, but being told *not* to say something amounted to the same as being told what *to* say. Manson obviously antagonized Hill, and it was clear he didn't like the lawyer who so frequently defended the felons and crooks that Manson wanted to see behind bars. Hill, under threat of contempt, kept control and didn't answer back.

Under intensive questioning, Noreen finally asked Hill if he really wanted the whole story. She didn't seem to think he would like it. Hill had been taken aback when she referred to her conversations with police about Gordon's alleged statement that he needed $2,000 for a bribe. Noreen told the lawyer that the police had talked about him. "They said it was an underhanded way of you getting $2,000 more out of Gordon. The police said that such an amount would be too small for a bribe and that a much larger amount would be needed in such a situation. It would have to be much larger—$2,000 is nothing in a bribe like that. They told me not to dare mention it," she added.

She had brought it up, however, and despite the obvious seriousness of such a suggestion, the surprised lawyer didn't explore the subject at length. He apparently decided that pressing further into the matter might encourage even more outrageous claims and extraneous evidence from the erratic Noreen. Hill then turned to the matter of the police questioning of witnesses in the case, complaining that some of it seemed unusual and possibly out of order. Manson observed that the police had every right to interview anybody they thought might have some knowledge of the crime.

When Hill claimed, "This story you have told us concerning Gordon is a falsification," Noreen firmly denied it. She wouldn't budge, asserting, "I spoke the truth to the best of my knowledge." She said she paid 30-minute visits twice a week to see her husband at Oakalla Prison. "Every time I went out I got all upset, and he just told me to tell the truth," she stated, adding that Inspector Horton sat in on one of the visits.

Cross-examined by Le Page, Carey's lawyer, Noreen was asked about the charge against Gordon in the bank holdup. "Was Jimmy involved in that robbery?" he asked. She answered, "Oh no, we didn't need money for that purpose, oh no, sir." She explained that when Carey came to the Burnaby apartment where she was staying the day after the shooting, he sat down beside the baby and cried. "He was just sick to think that the baby and I were there in that car," she added, although she had testified that he had taken a gun with him to the car when they left on the outing.

When Noreen's testimony ended and despite her denials, spectators were convinced that she had received one of the better deals made by the Vancouver police. She had been in the car, she had made the mask, she had been aware of the guns, and she had given the warning of the following police car. She could have been charged as an accomplice, but she gave the evidence the police needed, despite her assertions of threats and instructions about what she was to say and not say in the witness box. She was only too happy to help point the finger at the cops' main target, Joe Gordon. Her deal to try to save Carey had been made.

When Bob Smith took the witness stand, one thing crossed the minds of everyone in the room. His 6-foot 4-inch height was an instant reminder of eyewitness testimony that one of the men they saw at Watkins Winram was much taller than the other. Smith towered over both Gordon and Carey. Those who knew him realized he had lost a lot of weight, and he admitted that he had dropped some 30 pounds from his usual 220. Asked by Hill during cross-examination if the loss was because of worry about his involvement in the murder, Smith replied, "No worry, but thinking an awful lot about it." His concerns were compounded by the fact that after he was initially picked up, Mrs. Nielsen identified him in a police line-up. She said Smith was about the same height as the man she saw. It was interesting, but it wasn't positive identification.

Smith, an ex-soldier and ex-con with a long criminal record, had readily admitted to police that he had been at the murder scene and that he had driven the getaway convertible. A statement by Noreen that she had heard the police say they needed Smith as a material witness made it obvious that he would also benefit from a deal, despite all the denials. Like Noreen Carey, he wasn't charged with anything.

Smith, who knew Gordon because of the time they had spent together in jail, told Schultz that he met the accused pair the night before the murder. He firmly denied that they had cased a downtown office for a future break-in, but scepticism ran through the crowded courtroom when Smith said he had met Gordon by accident while out in his car. He contended that Gordon told him he was driving the Careys to dinner "and I got in for the ride." Smith denied seeing any weapons in the car or putting a .45 under the seat. He insisted that he stayed in the car when they reached Watkins Winram, while Joe and Jimmy got out.

His account was close to Noreen's. After they heard shots and the two others jumped in, he drove off "as fast as I could go." When Noreen spotted the following police car, he said Gordon became almost hysterical and shouted he wanted to get out, repeating, over and over, "Let me out! I shot the guy!" The impassive Gordon, listening intently, seemed a far cry from the man Smith described as having a case of hysterics when pursued by police.

Prosecutor Schultz asked the witness if he had told Noreen what to say. Smith replied, "She asked me afterwards what I thought she should say, but I told her I couldn't help her." Asked again if he had made any deals with the police, Smith firmly denied that he had. Cross-examined by Hill, the witness also denied that he threatened to harm Noreen if she said anything to police about his getting out of the car at Watkins Winram. He also contended that he hadn't seen the .45 revolver in the convertible.

Smith admitted to having tried to wipe away fingerprints before he and Noreen abandoned the getaway car. He told the jurors that he didn't know anything about a killing until he heard it later on his car radio while he was driving the woman and baby to her friends' place in Burnaby. Smith said Carey came to where he was working the next day and asked where his wife was.

While the trial continued, the furor about the one-man patrol cars and the crime wave went on. The *Sun* interviewed an American expert who had a different view from the one prevailing in Vancouver. Charles S. James, from Chicago, said the system generally worked well. He stated that it allowed more cars and more police to be out in the streets, but was only successful if police radio dispatchers were well trained and experienced in moving cars around in emergency situations. There was no evidence that Vancouver's badly trained force fit this bill. In the still-surging crime wave, two masked and armed bandits got away with $5,000 in a bank holdup in which an "attractive young woman" again was identified as the getaway driver. There seemed to be no other kind of female criminal in Vancouver!

At the trial, Brookes and Wiebe, the first two policemen on the scene, repeated their previous testimony. Schultz wanted Brookes to lie down on the courtroom floor to demonstrate to the jurors the position in which Sinclair had been found. Manson refused to allow this demonstration, stating that the request should have been made when they visited the actual site.

Of critical importance was the time that Fred Healey, operator of Arrow Cleaners on West Broadway, had seen Gordon on the night of December 7. He testified that Gordon, an acquaintance of his, came to his premises about 7:15 or 7:25 p.m. and asked for a favour. He wanted a drive to the east end, around 54th and Nanaimo, and Healey agreed to take him. Healey said that a few days later he got a call from somebody whose name sounded like "Joe Peet." He added, "I have no doubt somebody was trying to intimidate me. I received more than one call from 'Joe Peet.'" Healey said the caller stressed that it was actually 8:30 p.m. when he saw Gordon and asked if the police had put any pressure on Healey regarding his evidence. Healey, another witness with a police record, said he replied, "I told him yes, in a way they had, and that I would not be down there [police headquarters] of my own volition. I said the time was 7:15 or 7:25 and that was all I knew and hung up." Schultz told Manson that other witnesses had been receiving calls, but didn't elaborate. Healey bristled when Hill asked him about his record, angrily stating it was a long time ago and he had paid his debt to society.

Mrs. Elizabeth Hood, a seamstress at Arrow Cleaners, backed up Healey's evidence as to when Gordon called, but she made another significant comment. Mrs. Hood noticed that Gordon was wearing brown shoes splattered with mud. Lamont had found a pair of shoes matching this description wrapped up in the parcel seized during the arrest in the Burrard Street suite.

Of all the sleazy characters who participated at the murder trial, James Miller, alias McKenzie, undoubtedly was the worst. He was the man who had earlier testified that he was too busy shooting dope to take police to the .38 Webley hidden at the gospel hall. A convicted addict and trafficker, grey-haired Miller chewed gum vigorously and looked nervous as he entered the box. He was well aware of what Gordon's pals and the underworld in general would think of the evidence he was to give. Brought from Oakalla Prison under police escort, he amazed the audience with a recital of his record. He readily admitted to three drug offences, two sentences for armed robbery—one for ten years and one for three years, two sentences for car theft—one of a year's duration and one for fifteen months, and several other minor offences. Miller repeated that he obtained the gun for Gordon in order to repay a drug debt, leaving it in the hotel room of a man named Jimmy McKenzie.

Shortly after the killing, while he was behind bars in Oakalla Prison, awaiting an appearance on his latest drug offence, Miller said he had asked detectives Laurie McCullough and Al Steen to visit him. Gordon once more showed no emotion as he listened to the damning evidence of another informant. While Miller was quick to claim that no deal had been made, he also testified that he had told the detectives, "If you can get me out of here, I might be able to get you the gun." Miller had then appeared in court before Magistrate Gordon Scott and was released on his own recognizance.

When he was out of jail, Miller said he met Gordon about December 15 in a beer parlour. Gordon said he still had the gun and Miller asked for it back, saying, "I got to make some money to settle a beef of my own." The accused told him to look under the old stump at the gospel hall. Miller said Gordon also asked him to bring back a pair of gloves that he had left at the crime scene. Miller said he didn't find the gun on the first trip, but recovered the gloves, which he gave to Gordon. After a day spent shooting dope, he took Lamont back to the stump at the gospel hall, where they found the .38 Webley.

Manson and Hill were again at loggerheads when the defence lawyer asked Miller about the deal that got him out on his own recognizance. Miller denied any deal, but admitted that he had never before heard of anybody with a record like his getting out on his own word, particularly on a drug charge. When Hill asked again if he had a long record, Miller replied, almost proudly, "Oh, definitely." As Hill continued, Manson jumped in to protect his old colleague, Magistrate Scott, who had issued Miller's release. He accused the lawyer of inferring that Scott was guilty of "improper influence in the imposing of a sentence." It was obvious to everyone that this was true, not only in the freeing of Miller on his own recognizance, but also in imposing a lighter sentence on his latest drug charge. Manson insisted this wasn't so.

As he left the witness box on his way back to jail to finish his six months, Miller commented to his RCMP escort, "Same way back, I guess." He avoided looking at Gordon and Carey as he walked out of the courtroom. Miller left Vancouver quickly after serving his time, well aware that having broken the code of the underworld, his life could be forfeited.

Controversial policeman Pete Lamont told the court about the apprehension of Joe Gordon on December 7 at one of the apartments Gordon was known to frequent, on Burrard Street. He testified that police forensic specialists had identified the mud on the shoes he seized as identical to that in the area of the fuel plant; of course, the same mud could be found in many places. There was another clash between Manson and Hill when Gordon's lawyer asked Lamont about an interview he had had with the accused at the Palms Hotel early in the investigation. Schultz jumped in, claiming that this was inadmissible. Hill slid in the point he wanted to make regardless, claiming ingeniously, "I was going to ask the witness if he said he was going to frame Gordon." Manson exploded and said he wanted the question struck from the record. The jurors had heard it, but the judge told them to ignore it—something that is not easy to do. The jurors were dismissed from the room during the legal argument about admissibility that followed. Manson ruled the question inadmissible. Schultz pointed out, however, that once it was asked it was on the record, so he preferred that the jurors hear Lamont's response. Manson agreed; the jurors returned, and Lamont gave his answer: "No." He hadn't threatened to frame Gordon with Sinclair's murder.

Superintendent Jack Horton made a brief appearance, saying only that he knew Noreen Carey. To the surprise of most spectators, the defence lawyers asked no questions about her claims that he had threatened to take away her baby if she didn't testify as the police wanted—she was not to mention Smith getting out of the car, however briefly, at Watkins Winram. The investigators hadn't wanted this mentioned because it clouded the case against Gordon and Carey. The defence didn't ask about it, despite its apparent importance.

Another prosecution prizewinner was Jack McKenzie, a tough 45-year-old with a weathered face. He had been flown to Vancouver the day before, from a logging camp up the British Columbia coast at Kelsey Bay, to testify as a Crown witness. Miller had previously stated that he took Gordon to McKenzie's room at the Anchor Hotel and showed him the .38 Webley, which was in a bedside dresser drawer. McKenzie flatly denied any knowledge of the gun—with good reason, it was learned. Spectators were hushed as McKenzie, under Schultz's questioning, admitted that he had a record for murder. He had been an accomplice in a 1927 murder and had spent a long time in jail before being paroled. The parole was still in effect; McKenzie knew well that it could be revoked and he would find himself back in the penitentiary if he admitted anything about a gun. His evidence was no help at all to Schultz. McKenzie did admit that at one time he *had* had a gun, a Luger, when he was at a logging camp many years earlier.

Schultz wound up the case for the Crown, which depended largely on the evidence of the flaky Noreen Carey and Bob Smith, who admitted they had been at the Watkins Winram plant when Sinclair was gunned down. Smith's height presented a prosecution problem. While eyewitnesses had testified that one of the two men they saw was much taller than the other, they couldn't identify Smith as one of the two. Two other prosecution witnesses, Miller and McKenzie, were untrustworthy. But Miller admitted to having got the gun for Gordon, testifying that it had been in McKenzie's hotel room, and finally led the investigators to the murder weapon. It was the grimmest of the exhibits that lay on the courtroom table.

Now the battle belonged to Gordon and Carey. Even their pals, who had sat through the hearings, thought the jig was up for the pair. It was difficult to imagine how the accused could refute the damning evidence the jury had heard or what kind of alibi could be presented. Only the next few days would tell. Was it to be a walk to freedom or to the gallows?

THE CASE
FOR THE DEFENCE

AS A VOICE IN THE WILDERNESS CRYING FOR AID, TEENAGERS
PLEAD FOR HELP, BUT THERE IS NONE TO LEND A HELPING HAND.
NO LIFELINE IS THROWN; NO ASSURANCE OR COMFORT GIVEN. IT
IS SURVIVAL OF THE FITTEST AND SELF PRESERVATION FIRST.

—Excerpt from Joe Gordon's final message

On Monday, April 23, the eleventh day of the trial, it was finally the defence's turn. The jurors had heard 42 hours of testimony, strange tales, and contradictions from questionable witnesses who were generally strangers to the truth. They had listened to the damaging words of Noreen Carey and Bob Smith, who both claimed that Joe Gordon had wanted to get out of the getaway car as it was pursued by police because he had "shot the guy." Still, many questions remained: Were their accounts just desperate attempts to save their own necks? Would the deals they had made with the police allow them to wriggle free of any charges? Were Noreen's stories largely fantasies designed solely to try to save Jimmy from the death penalty? Was everything a fabrication?

Norman Mullins, Carey's co-counsel, claimed that no case had been established against his client and contended that the murder charge should be dismissed. Manson immediately rejected Mullins' proposition, saying that the issue would be left for the jury to decide. Mullins was followed by Hill, who quickly captured the moment when he said he would prove it couldn't have been Gordon who killed Sinclair.

His case would show that his client was downtown on Granville Street at 5:45 p.m. on the night of December 7, not in the east end, as Noreen and Smith claimed, and never, at the time of the crime, anywhere near the Watkins Winram fuel plant. He jolted the court and heightened the drama when he added, "We will also show, I think conclusively, that not only did Gordon not kill the policeman but who did." Spectators looked at each other and wondered who it could be. Would he try to finger Carey or Smith or even, hard as it was to believe, Noreen?

Hill's case soon became clear, but it was far from completely credible. Ten defence witnesses trooped into the courtroom or were delivered in handcuffs under police escort. They had a great deal in common; only one didn't have a criminal record. She was Lillian Middlecoat, Gordon's seventeen-year-old girlfriend. She had come to the attention of police because she worked in an amusement arcade on Granville Street that was frequented by ex-cons, bookies, bootleggers, hookers, and youths on the fringe of trouble with the law. The "Hall of Fun" had pinball machines, a coffee shop, and—the big attraction for its unsavoury clientele—a shooting gallery. Middlecoat, although only a teenager, liked the company of men well known to the police, including some very tough characters with long records of violence. At the arcade, she could not avoid being under police surveillance.

Middlecoat was red-haired, well-built, husky-voiced, and amazingly poised. As she testified at the life-or-death trial, every eye was focussed on her. The audience weighed every word she uttered and tried to interpret every gesture. The girl never wavered in telling her story in defence of her much older boyfriend and of the life she had lived in the several months since they met, probably at the "Hall of Fun." She spoke clearly and without hesitation, claiming that she and Gordon had been together on the afternoon of December 7 in a room at the Palms Hotel, the one Gordon shared with a drug dealer named Mac Ramsay. Ramsay and Gordon were old friends who had met in jail when they were about sixteen. The Palms on Granville Street in downtown Vancouver was a small, cheap, hotel-cum-rooming house favoured by visiting loggers and other transients. On the day in question, Middlecoat added, they and Ramsay made a trip to the main Vancouver police station to pick up a car that police were holding. It belonged to a friend of Gordon's.

After dropping Ramsay off, they then drove to a lane near Gordon's mother's home on West Fourteenth. She said her boyfriend had hoped to see his brother, but when he didn't arrive within a half-hour they drove back downtown. The witness recounted that they then visited the La Salle Club on Granville Street, where Gordon played pool while she sat in the coffee shop. Her tale became slightly confusing as she tried to explain how they went next to a nearby parking lot and switched cars because Joe wanted to drive a convertible. Middlecoat said her boyfriend then drove her to her apartment to pick up a sweater before she went back to work at the pinball parlour. Asked by Hill what time this was, she said she looked at the clock on the nearby Belmont Hotel and it was about ten minutes after six, the time at which Noreen Carey and Smith claimed she and the others were driving with Gordon from the east end to downtown. Middlecoat stuck to her story under cross-examination.

Following graphic testimony and technical details about the actual gunning down of Sinclair, Hill introduced the most dramatic moments in the trial. Lawyers, spectators, and even court officials were spellbound as Hill announced he would prove who had actually murdered the policeman. Into the witness box stepped Mac Ramsay, Gordon's roommate, who admitted to eight convictions in the previous ten years, ranging from a $25 fine to three years in the penitentiary for theft. An excited whisper ran through the startled crowd when he named Herbert Howerton, a dead man, as the killer. The 23-year-old Korean War veteran and one-time prison guard had been fatally shot by Bud Johnstone of the RCMP earlier in the month during a blazing gun battle in Coquitlam. He had been the leader of a four-man gang that toted an arsenal of deadly weapons. Now Hill's defence claimed that in December Howerton had also slain Gordon Sinclair. Onlookers stared at each other in amazement, and reporters at the crowded press table scribbled furiously before dashing out to phone in the sensational news to city desks and radio stations.

The shoot-out at Coquitlam had made headlines across the province. As a result, there were few people in the courtroom who didn't connect the name Howerton with the dead gunman in the parking lot outside the bank. Howerton was gone, but three members of his gang were still in custody. Ramsay said the holdup man and Al Stromson, a habitué of 1350 Burrard Street, had come to the room at the Palms Hotel the night before Sinclair's murder. He didn't say much more, but naming Howerton was enough. Hill would present other evidence to back his case that Sinclair's slayer was a man now dead and buried. Ramsay made a few final comments, telling the court that at about 6:15 to 6:30 p.m. on December 7, he saw Joe Gordon rushing up the front steps of the hotel. He also recalled that the style-conscious Gordon was dressed in black that night.

Mrs. Louise Stromson also pointed the finger at Howerton. She said that a few days before December 7 a man resembling Howerton had come to the apartment on Burrard where she was living. She told the jurors that he was slightly built, of medium height with curly, brownish hair, and bore a resemblance to Gordon. As the woman testified, she looked directly at Gordon, who stared back at her with no sign of recognition. The woman added that Gordon had phoned the night of the murder about 10:50 p.m. to say he was coming over. He arrived about 11:30 p.m.

The defence then called Francis Joseph Dale, 22, and Donald Ian Rutledge, 24, who were brought into the courtroom handcuffed to RCMP escorts. Dale was in Oakalla pending his appeal against a five-year sentence for breaking and entering. Rutledge, who occupied a cell nearby, was serving six months for possession of an unregistered weapon. Rutledge said he was in the Burrard Street suite when a man named "Ed" came in and gave Stromson a gun, a .38 Webley. Dale testified that he saw Gordon on the night of the killing at about 6 p.m. in the York Hotel beer parlour, at Robson and Howe in downtown Vancouver. There were snickers from spectators when Schultz asked if Dale had known Gordon at Oakalla and Dale answered, "I have seen him in church on Sunday."

Two survivors of the Coquitlam gun battle were the next to be escorted into court; they also wore handcuffs. William Gary Owen and William Edwin Banks were in prison awaiting trial. Their story was that they were in a car with Howerton about 10 p.m. on

December 7 when they saw Gordon on a downtown street. They claimed Howerton stopped and passed a brown-paper–wrapped parcel to the accused.

Another defence witness with a record was Jack MacArthur, who alleged that he met Howerton and another man in the Castle Hotel beer parlour on the evening of December 7, and they sat there until about 11 p.m. He claimed that Howerton left briefly, saying he wanted to get a newspaper to see if there was anything in it about a shooting. MacArthur's evidence confirmed that some members of the underworld were very well dressed. He couldn't remember exactly what Howerton was wearing that night because "he seemed to have a lot of clothes. Every time I saw him he was wearing something different. I never saw him in the same clothes twice."

Howerton's 51-year-old father testified that the pair of shoes found in the paper-wrapped parcel in Gordon's possession had belonged to his son. Earlier evidence had established that they were a size and a half larger than those normally worn by the deceased Howerton. The man broke into tears and missed the double meaning of his words when he was asked to identify a picture of his son. Holding it and looking at it for a long time, the senior Howerton sobbed, and nobody laughed when he said, "It looks like the dead image of Herb."

Schultz was quick with his cross-examination, as he was with all the defence witnesses. He obviously thought the jurors were capable of judging the worth of the stories they were hearing from the defence's star-studded lineup. Given Gordon's lifestyle, it could hardly be expected that he would have friends from local seminaries or learned professions testifying on his behalf. These were his creature companions from the underworld. The prosecutor also believed that the attempt to link Howerton to Sinclair's murder was a crude alibi that jurors would immediately see through and dismiss.

JOE GORDON TESTIFIES

THOSE POOR UNFORTUNATES WHO WERE TO BE MY FRIENDS
WELCOMED ME. WHY NOT? MISERY LOVES COMPANY. ALSO THE
MOST COMPASSIONATE PEOPLE ARE CRIMINALS FOR THEY HAVE
SUFFERED THE REJECTION OF SOCIETY.

—Excerpt from Joe Gordon's final message

The event that courtroom aficionados, regular attendees, the press, and the reading and listening public had been waiting for finally occurred on the twelfth day of the trial. Joe Gordon took the stand at 2:31 p.m. on Tuesday, April 24 to tell his story and fight for his life. Would bottled-up emotion finally spill over as he battled back against tough cross-examination from Schultz? Would there be a crack in Gordon's cool composure? Smith had testified that Gordon was near hysterics when he jumped into the car as they fled from Watkins Winram, but since then the accused murderer had always remained icily calm in public. He had been grilled for hours by Lamont and other detectives, but hadn't given an inch or admitted a thing. His face had never shown emotion—not a wince, not a sneer, not even a discernable smirk throughout his twelve days in court.

Gordon was turned out in a natty plum-coloured sports coat, white shirt, tie, grey trousers, and gleaming black shoes, a striking contrast to the grey suits he had worn previously in the dock and in direct contrast to the sombre tones prevailing in the room. He knew every eye was riveted on him as he took the oath and sat down in the witness box. He was an actor revelling in a role, with complete control of centre stage. Gordon was cocky and self-assured. He winked at Lillian Middlecoat, who sat in the public benches near the front of the courtroom. She smiled back.

Gordon threw up a stonewall defence, a denial of everything that had been stated in court, especially the assertions of Noreen Carey and Bob Smith. They had painted him as the instigator and leader of the trip to Watkins Winram, the man who had walked toward the plant's darkened office with a gun, and the man who later cried out that he had shot the guy. Under Hill's questioning, Gordon said he was nowhere near the scene of the shooting that night. He insisted that he simply wasn't at Watkins Winram despite what the other two had maintained. He claimed that he was in his hotel room at the time of the murder and was a victim of a massive conspiracy, the target of a police frame-up. He repeated several times that he wasn't there, so he couldn't have pulled the trigger and been the man who murdered Gordon Sinclair.

The accused man spoke in a steady, low voice, and like others on the stand before him, he was at times difficult to hear. The jurors again leaned forward trying to catch every word in a scene similar to the one created by Noreen Carey. Gordon repeated the evidence given by Middlecoat and then added that he drove the convertible to West Pender Street after taking Middlecoat to work. There he parked the vehicle and left the keys in the glove compartment, as he usually did when he borrowed it. He said a man named Bill Traynor was looking after the car while the actual owner was doing time in jail.

Gordon continued the recital of his movements. He said he went back to the Palms Hotel and returned to his room, where he stayed alone until shortly after eight. He then left and went to see Healey at his dry-cleaning establishment. The importance of the timing detailed in Healey's earlier evidence and the telephone threats Healey said he'd received concerning exactly what time Gordon had visited now became very apparent. It was obvious why someone had tried to get him to change his account. Healey had said Gordon arrived about 7:15 p.m., which was not long after Sinclair's murder. Now Gordon was maintaining that it was after eight when he showed up. This meant Healey would have agreed to drive him to Carey's apartment in the east end well after the time of Sinclair's death. There was no one at Carey's place, Gordon told the court, and he then went to see another friend, Al Stromson, at his Burrard Street apartment. It was here that Lamont and a police detachment arrested him.

Joe Gordon then brought the dead Howerton into the picture. He said that en route to Stromson's he met Howerton, who stopped as he was passing in a car. Asked by Hill what Howerton did, Gordon replied, "He gave me a parcel and a dollar bill." This was the brown-papered parcel containing a pair of shoes and pants that police seized at the apartment. Gordon said they were his. When asked how Howerton got them, Gordon said he'd loaned them to him the previous day. "He was going to have his pants and shoes repaired and I offered him mine," explained Gordon. Those in court remembered the evidence already given that Howerton, like Gordon, was a clotheshorse. Gordon's explanation did not ring true.

Gordon then linked the deceased bandit to the convertible, which he said could be picked up easily because the keys were always in the glove compartment. He claimed that earlier he had loaned the car to Howerton and Bob Smith, so they were also familiar with its availability. Gordon denied ever having seen the .38 that was shown to him in court.

Asked by Hill if he ever played Russian roulette, Gordon smiled and answered scornfully, "Of course not." He did admit, however, that he had experience with guns.

"Legally or illegally?" asked Hill.

"Illegally," answered Gordon. He also readily agreed that he had often been in trouble with the police. Responding to Judge Manson, Gordon said he had met Howerton on two previous occasions, once in Vancouver and once in Langley. He gave a physical description of the bank bandit that closely matched his own.

Gordon continued to deny Noreen Carey's evidence that he had been in her apartment and had driven the group to Watkins Winram. Hill asked him directly, "Did you shoot Constable Sinclair?"

Without hesitation Gordon answered, "Of course not." He made it clear that while he knew lots of policemen, he did not know

Sinclair. He added that he had been in lineups at police headquarters but had not been identified by any of the three eyewitnesses as one of the men they'd seen at the plant. Gordon said Pete Lamont interviewed him about five times before he was charged, and that was when the frame-up began.

With his entire defence based on the contention that he wasn't at the scene and therefore could not have pulled the trigger, Gordon's appearance was short and a disappointment to some who had expected more. It was all over in 62 minutes. Schultz took over cross-examination and was permitted to cite Gordon's arrest record. He detailed Gordon's long criminal career, without referring to his run-ins with juvenile authorities: October 1938, one year for possession of housebreaking tools, at the age of 17; April 1940, two years for car theft; January 1942, four years plus two concurrent for "violent stealing"; February 1946, five years for drug possession; March 1946, five years for car theft concurrent with the drug sentence; and March 1950, attempted robbery with violence, breaking and entering, possession of an offensive weapon, and retaining stolen property, six years concurrent on each charge plus five years concurrent for drug possession.

Gordon admitted he had only been released from penitentiary in March 1955. Since then he had lived as a gambler, except for a few weeks when he sold insurance policies on television sets. He also admitted that on occasion he was known as Joseph Mason and Jeffries Harris.

Schultz asked if he had tried to arrange an alibi with Betty Slack, a Palms Hotel employee who actually ran the premises, although she was listed as a maid. Gordon denied having attempted to get her to say the exact time he went to his room on the night of December 7 and the exact time that he left. He also maintained that he had lots of money and had never said anything to Noreen Carey about needing more for bribes on his bank-holdup charge.

Gordon finally showed emotion when he angrily asked Schultz how he was supposed to answer detailed questions about the killing when he hadn't been there and hadn't done it. He couldn't give a "yes" or "no" to the probing of the prosecutor. Hill jumped up, complaining, "The man says he wasn't there. This sort of ambiguous nonsense should be stopped."

Manson disagreed. He said there was nothing ambiguous or nonsensical about the questioning and stated that Schultz could continue. But Schultz got nowhere. Joe Gordon gave only flat denials. Asked about the scrape he'd had on his face when he was picked up, Gordon claimed he got it while fooling around with a man named Frankie Dale, who had accidentally clipped him. Schultz charged that Gordon actually got it while banging into a protruding waterspout on a building on Fifth Avenue when he was running from the murder scene. "I did not," Gordon replied defiantly, replacing his short burst of anger with a calm, cool response as Schultz continued the attack.

When the court rose for the day, Manson ordered Gordon held in tight custody. He was not to be allowed to talk to anyone, not even Hill, prior to his appearance the next day. His reappearance was much of the same: denial after denial of the accusations made by Schultz. Gordon left the box having admitted absolutely nothing, but he had managed to polish up his image as a dandy. In evidence, he had described with some pride what he was wearing on the night of December 7: "I was wearing a black suit, black overcoat, and suede shoes. And I was wearing a black hat that night." Reflecting on his dress, he told the jurors, "I am the type to wear black." Gordon stepped blithely from the box at the end of his testimony. He was cocky but probably less confident than he appeared. Gordon was too smart not to know that the jury would have trouble believing much of his evidence.

Gordon's shaky defence was hit hard when Schultz called Betty Slack of the Palms Hotel as a rebuttal witness, even though she also had a police record. She testified that five days after Sinclair's killing, Gordon told her he was in a jam and asked if she could help him. She said he asked her to tell police, if she was questioned, that he was in his room from about six to eight on the night of the slaying. The woman said there were others around who heard him make the request. Betty Slack shot a gaping hole in Gordon's story when she added that as far as she knew, he was not in his room at that time.

Schultz went out of his way to let the jury know that this woman had not been pressured to give her evidence. Asked by the prosecutor if the police had squeezed her, Slack replied with an emphatic "No."

Carey's lawyer had contended at the start of the trial that the Crown had no case against his client, but Manson had rejected the argument. After Gordon was dealt with, the court was told that the co-accused would not enter the box to testify. In light of the evidence that put Carey at the scene—particularly that of his wife—the line that there was no case against him caused some surprise. Carey, like Gordon, sat passively during all the contradictory evidence without showing any outward emotion.

Now the case moved quickly. Schultz gave a short summation, describing Gordon's defence as "concocted, untrue and a tissue of lies." He said the defence witnesses had tried to drag in "red herrings," and he reminded the jurors that only the girl, Middlecoat, was without a criminal record. The jurors had gathered, however, that she liked the company of crooks and their hangouts anywhere on East Hastings or lower Granville streets. The prosecutor dismissed the suggestion that the police had tried to frame Gordon, noting that the defence had had every opportunity to cross-examine Lamont and Horton about the mixed allegations and denials of deals that had been presented to the court, but they had not done so. Schultz stressed that they had turned down the chance and said also that leading investigators had not been called to rebut Noreen Carey's assertions that police threatened to take away her baby if she didn't testify the way they wanted her to. In addition, Schultz emphasized, the defence had asked no questions about the allegations that the prosecution wanted nothing said about Smith getting out of the car at the Watkins Winram plant. The defence had not pressed any of these points, repeated Schultz.

The prosecutor pointed to the bizarre presence of the baby in the car. Schultz said the infant was there in order to bolster the group's claim that they were out for a simple car ride, in case for some reason the police stopped them. The child was meant as a decoy, to emphasize that they were people on an innocent outing, far removed from any criminal plans or designs that night, Schultz argued.

Schultz dismissed attempts to blame Howerton for the crime, adding that it was simply a ploy to introduce as Sinclair's killer a man now dead, who could not appear to deny it. The story about the loaned shoes and pants was simply nonsense, he said. The prosecutor said Noreen had done her best to place the murder weapon in Gordon's hands. He reminded the jury of Smith's assertion that Gordon became hysterical and began shouting after Noreen saw the police car behind them. Schultz contended that Gordon's reaction proved he was the killer, because up to that point "they thought that when they disposed of Sinclair they were free. They were unaware, however, of another fact; the Nielsens were eyewitnesses who had seen two men acting suspiciously near Watkins Winram and had called police."

Hill gave a long summation, reiterating that Gordon had an alibi and witnesses who testified he could not have been the killer. He agreed that there had been a great welter of contradictory evidence, but he pointed to suggestions of his client being framed. Hill argued there had been tremendous police pressure on Noreen Carey and Bob Smith to finger Gordon. He recalled the talk of various deals being made to get the evidence needed to convict his client. He recounted that Smith had gone willingly to the plant and then driven the getaway car. "Why wasn't he charged equally with the two accused?" he asked. Gordon was a "calm and self-assured man," Hill argued. Did the jurors think that an admitted long-standing criminal like Gordon "would have been stupid enough to make the mistakes alleged to have been made after the killing?" he asked.

There was the evidence of the three eyewitnesses regarding the appearance and identity of the two men they saw walking toward the plant. The eyewitnesses were unanimous that one of the two men they saw was much taller than the other. Hill stressed what had been obvious to everyone in court: Gordon and Carey were the same height to within an inch, and Smith was about eight inches taller than either of them. Looking straight at the jurors, Hill stated: "Smith is involved in this case right up to his ears, and his ears would be over the heads of Gordon and Carey." Without doubt, the height factor was one of the few strong points in the defence argument. Smith certainly towered over the other two. But would it matter?

Derek Le Page's summation on Carey's behalf was much shorter. He too pointed out the height differences. He told the jurors that if they "decided that Gordon was the man, Carey could not have been the other, as he was about the same height." The key question, the lawyer stressed, was what the four had in mind when they left the Careys' apartment, taking the weeks-old infant with them. He argued that it was not to commit a crime. "These are the facts, that this man loved this baby, and at the time he left the house those were his feelings, not those of one out to commit an unlawful act," stated Le Page.

When he sat down, all that remained was Manson's charge to the jurors and their decision as to whether the accused should live or die. They had been sequestered in the Hotel Vancouver for more than two weeks. They had listened to 42 witnesses who produced 1,400 pages of transcript, viewed 60 exhibits, made a trip to the area of Watkins Winram and seen the old tree stump behind the gospel hall where the .38 Webley was recovered. They had heard completely contradictory evidence: the stories of Noreen Carey and Smith, and the total denial by Gordon that he was the killer. They had seen witnesses brought into the courtroom in handcuffs and listened to criminals with long records give versions of events leading up to the fatal night. One was an addict who had been too busy shooting dope to tell police what he knew; another was a paroled murderer who could have wound up back in the penitentiary if he told the whole truth about Gordon getting the .38. They knew Gordon had not buckled under relentless cross-examination, and they heard the prosecutor later contend that the story of the accused for the night of December 7 constituted a monstrous lie. They hadn't heard a word from Carey because he had declined to testify. This was later acknowledged to have been a bad tactical error.

Manson began his charge to the jury at 2:00 p.m. on Thursday, May 26, but as time wore on it became clear that it would take longer than the remainder of the day for him to finish his summation. He was later to apologize for erring in trying to end the trial that day, and it was unusual for Manson to apologize for anything. He dwelled at length on various points of law and the options presented to the jury in rendering its verdict. As he reviewed the evidence, he said it was clear that Noreen Carey's main interest was her husband, and it was the same for Gordon's girlfriend, Lillian Middlecoat. He noted that jurors had heard from friends of Gordon Sinclair and of the accused, and he told them they should not be carried away by the testimony of any one witness but should consider the case as a whole.

Manson cautioned that Noreen Carey had admitted frankly that her common-law husband was her interest. "You will keep this in mind when weighing her evidence," he said. "It doesn't follow that because a person has an interest they will perjure themselves, but it is inevitable that the temptation to commit perjury is there. There is no escaping that. It is for you to say if a witness has succumbed to that temptation."

There had been evidence given that the police had endeavoured to encourage Noreen to distort her evidence, he stated. Manson pointed out: "The question will arise as to whether Mrs. Carey and Robert Smith were accomplices in the crime of murder. We are not going to try them, but it is important for you to determine whether or not they are accomplices." If it was concluded that they were accomplices, Manson stressed, then their evidence would have to be treated with special caution. He described an accomplice as anyone "who knowingly and voluntarily co-operated with, aided, assisted, advised, or encouraged another in the commission of a crime." He cautioned the jury, "If you find that Mrs. Carey was an accomplice, and that Smith was also, evidence of one cannot corroborate that of the other."

The judge added that Mrs. Carey was a difficult witness and pointedly observed what everybody already knew: "This lady seems to be rather familiar with crime. She knew about Russian roulette. She knew about guns. She knew how to make a mask and after making it she went willingly with her gun-toting husband and his friend and took her baby along for the ride ... It is for you to decide whether or not she is an accomplice and possibly guilty of murder." The judge added, "Is she telling the truth or is she trying to pin the crime on Gordon and exculpate Carey?" He wondered how much credence could be given her story when it came to her husband. "She was going to say that Smith got out, but changed her story as this was inconvenient as Smith drove them away," Manson stated.

Manson reminded the jurors that accusations had been made about the actions of Superintendent Horton and Inspector Lamont and about possible evidence tampering, but emphasized that the defence lawyers had declined to cross-examine them at any length on these matters. Allegations about threats and taking away the baby therefore went unanswered. Referring to the presence of the baby in the car, Manson asked, "Was she a decoy if they were stopped by the police, just a family party on its way?" The judge said that all his remarks about Gordon applied generally to Carey and that jurors must draw their own conclusions as to why he fled Vancouver, leaving his wife and child behind.

He asked the jurors if Gordon did not impress them "as one rather proud of his record, boastful, a big-bad-wolf type." Manson said the jurors' first duty was to accept or reject Gordon's alibi, and any doubt they had about him being at the scene must be resolved in his favour. They must consider Gordon's alibi and the testimony of his witnesses. Manson pointed out the defence assertion that Noreen Carey's evidence was a falsehood and reiterated that Hill had referred to the discrepancies in the accounts of the witnesses who saw the men in the lane at Watkins Winram. Manson cited the defence claims that there was insufficient evidence to show that Gordon was at the site, although Noreen Carey's and Bob Smith's evidence placed him there.

Referring to the evidence of Gordon's girlfriend Lillian Middlecoat, Manson opined, "It is hard to understand why a girl of seventeen thinks it is worthwhile to get mixed up with a man with a record such as Gordon but it is none of our business." He said Middlecoat testified to a timetable that, if it was believed, meant Gordon could not have been at Watkins Winram when the policeman was killed. There was also evidence from Gordon contending that Howerton had done the shooting. The judge said of that evidence: "Howerton is dead and cannot speak for himself."

Carey's defence, Manson continued, was that it had not been proven that he was with Gordon when the murder was committed.

"He takes the position that if he was one of the men, they were doing no more than 'casing' the job and had not entered upon an attempt and that there was no attempted robbery." Manson also referred again to the eyewitnesses' evidence regarding the difference in height of the men they saw at the scene.

The judge then explained the legal position of the two accused. If they formed a common purpose, and one of them in carrying it out committed an offence, each was party to the offence. "It can't be manslaughter," stated the judge. "Throughout this case, it is murder or not."

Manson had started his charge at 2:00 p.m. and it didn't end until almost nine o'clock, after several breaks, including more than two hours for dinner. It had been a very long day. He told the jurors he had erred in trying to end the trial that day and that the long hours had put everyone under considerable strain. As the jurors filed out to ponder the verdicts that could mean life or death for the pair, neither Gordon nor Carey showed any sign of stress as they were led down the stairs to the holding cells to await their fate. As he left, Gordon nodded to a friend who was sitting near the front of the room. Middlecoat was gone, having fled the courtroom in tears during Manson's long charge. Noreen Carey was staying with friends.

It had been one of the most sensational trials in Vancouver's history and at the time was thought to be the longest murder case ever tried in B.C. courts. Despite the long hours and with no knowledge of how long the jury might take to reach its verdict, few budged from the public benches. They were not prepared to give up their seats and miss the last act of the drama that had unfolded before them for more than two weeks. The police, the press, and the spectators mulled over the evidence as they waited. The general impression was that the prosecution had demolished Gordon's hard-to-believe alibi. It also was hard to accept as gospel the stories given by the cons and ex-cons who had testified on his behalf. The evidence about the acquisition of the gun appeared far-fetched, but there seemed little doubt that Gordon had given directions as to where to find the murder weapon under the old tree stump behind the gospel hall, despite his contention that he had never seen the weapon. There were lingering doubts about Noreen Carey and Bob Smith, who obviously had accepted immunity from the police in exchange for their evidence. The dry cleaner's evidence about the exact time he saw Gordon and the alleged phone threats was significant. There also was the testimony of Betty Slack about events and timing at the Palms Hotel, plus her evidence that Gordon had asked her to commit perjury by saying he was in his room during the crucial hours on December 7. She had demolished that vital part of the defence, her evidence making it clear that Gordon was not at the Palms at the time Sinclair died. The only real puzzle was the question of height, the positive assertions of the two reliable eyewitnesses that one of the two men they saw was much taller than the other, and Bob Smith, of course, fit this bill.

Speculation boiled for only a short time. About midnight, the jurors told the sheriff they were ready to return with their verdict. Lawyers and reporters scrambled back to their seats. Among the spectators who had waited tensely for the end of the tragedy was young Ian Sinclair, whose father had been slain. He sat with a family friend, having left his distraught mother and sisters at home. The courtroom again was packed as police brought Gordon and Carey up the stairs from the cells. Gordon still wore his plum-coloured jacket and Carey wore a grey suit. The jurors, who had retired at 9:12 p.m., returned in under three hours at 12:06 a.m. Those in the courtroom watched closely as they filed in, wondering if it was true that if the jurors didn't look at the accused, they had found them guilty. They gave away nothing on this occasion. Some glanced quickly at Gordon and Carey as they took their seats, and some didn't.

The jury spokesman said they had reached a decision, and the accused were ordered to stand. Within seconds a nervous-sounding foreman gave the verdict. Gordon heard his fate first. "Guilty." He didn't blanch and in a show of bravado gave a wide smile and a wink to the crowded reporters' table. It was different for Carey, whose body swayed slightly as he waited to hear his fate. His eyes blinked rapidly, and the word "guilty" obviously stunned him. His normally pale face turned ashen as he slumped back into his seat. Carey seemed unaware of Manson's mournful words, but Gordon smiled widely again as the judge intoned, "You will be held until July 10 when you will be taken to a place of execution and hanged by the neck until you are dead." In the seconds of icy silence that followed his words, a male voice from the spectators' benches said quietly but firmly, "Amen."

Lead investigators Lamont and McCullough were among those on hand to hear the sentence of death. Their faces registered nothing as they heard the penalty imposed on the men they had wanted so badly and hunted so steadfastly. As the pair left the dock, Gordon offered Carey a package of cigarette papers and tobacco, seemingly no longer angry that his cohort had been a police informant. His view was to change.

A few minutes after Gordon and Carey were sentenced, an unemotional voice broke into the police radio frequency, relaying the news to officers in patrol cars as it had with the news of Sinclair's death. The voice said simply that Gordon and Carey had been found guilty. Sinclair's colleagues had waited almost a year and a half for the verdict they wanted. It was close to 1:00 a.m., but a large crowd waited outside the courtroom as the handcuffed, convicted murderers walked the few steps to a waiting van that whisked them off to Oakalla Prison. There remained only two months until their date with the hangman.

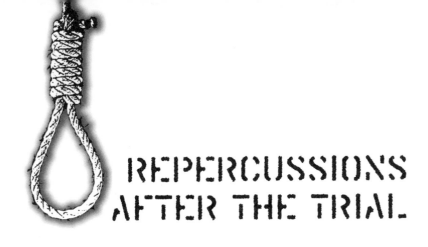

REPERCUSSIONS AFTER THE TRIAL

PUBLIC SERVANTS AREN'T INTERESTED IN GUILT OR INNOCENCE,
THEIR SOLE INTEREST LIES IN CONVICTION.

—*Excerpt from Joe Gordon's final message*

If Lillian Middlecoat had tears for Joe Gordon, his mother certainly did not. When a *Vancouver Sun* reporter arrived at her home the morning after her son was sentenced to die, she didn't let him in but spoke from an upstairs window of her home on Fourteenth Avenue. She was very definite and direct in her answers to his questions, and any suggestions of motherly love went out the window, so to speak. Seemingly without any affection for her son, who was due soon to dangle at the end of a rope, she said, "He made his own bed and now let him lie in it." She said Joe wouldn't come home when the family wanted him to, "so why should we go to him now?" Without remorse, she added: "Joe isn't part of the family any more … all my boys are good boys, respectable, all but Joe. He would go off with his friends, those bandit friends. That was the life Joe wanted and that was the life he had. It wasn't a life with his family." With these harsh, bitter words on the fate of her son, Joe Gordon's mother pulled back and slammed the window shut. She had four other sons and three daughters.

A friend of Noreen's told reporters of a note that Carey had written to her during the trial.

I love Noreen and my little Lesley too much to put them through the suffering that a jail visit would mean. I just cannot tell you how much it means to me that you are looking out for Noreen and little Lesley—that is something that I myself will never be able to show my gratitude for. Not being able to look out for them myself it certainly is a relief to know someone like you is around to help her and the baby. However there is one thing more I want to ask you if it is in your power to do. Please try to keep Noreen away from the courtroom on the day the verdict is reached. Should I happen to be unlucky when the verdict is handed down it would be better if I never saw Noreen again.

Noreen Carey *wasn't* in the courtroom to hear the decision; she was staying at a friend's home. Crying bitterly and clutching the baby, she told reporters that the first thing she wanted was to see Carey— "the man I love and I will always love." She sobbed when she was told that he was already in one of the death-row cells. "I have learned from my minister to have faith and that the truth will come out in the end," Noreen added. She told reporters that a special prayer service was to be held at the Baptist church she was attending.

With only two months until the date of execution, lawyers studied the trial transcript and planned their appeals. On May 2 it was reported that Ottawa was having problems with the July 10 execution date for Gordon and Carey because two other death penalties were due to be imposed elsewhere in Canada on the same day, one in Manitoba and the other in Ontario. Officials said it was likely, however, that appeals on behalf of the West Coast pair would mean a change of date. It was disclosed for the first time that, contrary to the popular view, there actually were two Canadian hangmen, one living in Ontario, the other in Quebec. Officials in Ottawa said the hangmen got $200 to $400 for each execution, depending on how far they had to travel. Not surprisingly, the Quebec hangman had recently told a parliamentary committee that he had trouble keeping assistants: Toward the time when they were to attend their first execution, most of them changed their minds and quit.

Although it didn't affect them on death row, Gordon and Carey watched and heard the near-riot that soon developed at Oakalla. It happened when appeals of twenty-year sentences for three of the drug-gang members who smashed Kinna's legs—Tremblay, Frenette and Talbot—were turned down by the provincial court. They grabbed a guard, held him hostage with a razor at his throat, and demanded their case be reviewed. After six tense hours and with a promise that their case would be studied further, they released the guard. Eventually the Supreme Court of Canada refused to consider their appeal and new sentences were imposed for the hostage taking, the time to be served concurrent with the twenty years already imposed.

Complaints from the public about the increasing number of escaped, desperate, and violent criminals back on the street became louder and more numerous, and pleas for action were echoed in the media. Finally, in Victoria, Attorney General Robert Bonner announced that Oakalla would be converted to a maximum-security prison when a new jail was opened in Haney in 1957. He hoped this would reduce the number of escapees.

On May 16 Larry Hill filed Gordon's appeal. The notice was short and maintained that Manson had failed to put his client's defence claims about the alibi and the witnesses who swore to it to the jury properly. Carey's appeal, making the same argument, was submitted a few days later.

While they awaited the outcome of their appeals, Gordon and Carey heard the trapdoor above the elevator shaft at Oakalla crash one more time as a fellow inmate on death row was hanged. The chill of horror that ran through the men on death row can only be imagined. The executions took place only a few feet from the cells where the condemned lived. Robert Graham, 24, a miner, was executed for the senseless, drunken, kicking death of a 21-year-old in a Kitsilano parking lot. Many people felt he should have been convicted of manslaughter and imprisoned, not found guilty of murder and sentenced to die. Graham went to his doom with "love and kindness in his heart" after finding religion. In a farewell note he urged his parents: "Please go to church regularly." They told reporters he was a good boy until he fell in with the wrong crowd.

Graham even sent a letter to Supreme Court Judge J.O. Wilson, thanking him for a fair trial. Prison chaplain Grant Hollingsworth said Graham quickly received a "very nice reply." Two men benefitted directly from the miner's death: their failing eyesight improved with the corneas he donated in a final gesture of atonement. Their relatives profusely thanked Graham's parents.

In early June, City Hall officials said several claims had been filed for the $6,000 reward offered for information in Sinclair's murder; $5,000 came from the city, and $1,000 personally from Mayor Hume. They stated that final disposition would have to wait until all possible appeals had been dealt with.

Relatives sobbed hysterically and one had to be helped from court when tough justice brought down 25-year sentences for the three survivors of the bank holdup in which Howerton died in a hail of police bullets. Judge Bruce Fraser told Owen, Foster, and Banks that he didn't believe their contention that before setting out on the bank job they had no intention of actually using their weapons. The judge pointed out that their arsenal included submachine guns, although they had not been used. "The protection of the public is of prime importance," he said, jolting the young trio with the quarter-century terms, although they took it more stoically than many of their relatives in the crowded courtroom.

They paid a heavy price for a holdup planned in a beer parlour. Foster said Howerton had talked him into it. Banks said he didn't know about the submachine guns until they arrived at the scene and realized they were in the van. He said there was an agreement that they would not fire their weapons unless absolutely necessary, and then only over people's heads. Judge Fraser didn't buy any of it. He told the three, "It was well-planned down to the assembly of weapons, provision of disguises, and the stealing of a getaway car."

The Vancouver Police Commission got its fourth commissioner, which the Tupper report on the Mulligan affair had recommended, with the provincial government's appointment of another military man, this time an ex-sailor. He was local businessman J. Douglas

Maitland, Canada's most decorated naval hero of the Second World War. Maitland rose to lieutenant commander and won the Distinguished Service Cross and Bar for service in torpedo boats in the Mediterranean and Adriatic seas. On being appointed he quipped, "The only experience I have had with the police is being tagged for parking."

On June 13, at Schultz's request, Manson agreed to postpone the execution date of Gordon and Carey until October 16 pending their appeals, which were now expected to be heard early in the fall.

New swivel-hipped entertainer Elvis Presley filled the news pages again when Vancouver authorities worried about the effect his gyrations would have on youngsters and whether or not it would lead them down the slippery slope to degradation and, ultimately, crime. In Presley's first major television appearance on *The Ed Sullivan Show,* the cameras were allowed to show the entertainer only from the hips up. Presley's influence and rock'n'roll itself caused a frenzy when Bill Haley and His Comets attracted some 5,000 teenagers to a show. *Sun* critic Stanley Bligh solemnly labelled the music "the ultimate in musical depravity" and a threat to youngsters, both physically and morally. A University of B.C. psychology professor dubbed the event a mass narcotic. Musician Haley agreed that youngsters in the Kerrisdale Arena should not have been up off their seats, rocking and dancing, but pointed out, "Man, with that kind of beat, how can you stop them?" Even veteran jazzman-trumpeter Louis Armstrong was wrong on rock'n'roll. He laughed at the worries when interviewed during a Vancouver visit and thought the furor was nonsense. He predicted, wrongly, it was a fad that wouldn't last.

Presley's name was raised in Port Alberni on Vancouver Island in relation to an actual crime when two youths testified that they got enraged because their dates wouldn't stop talking about the singer. They dumped the girls, picked up two more, and went to a graveyard, where they dug up the body of a recently buried man and dragged it along the ground with chains latched to their truck. Two-year sentences were eventually handed down, but the girls were found not guilty after they stressed they hadn't gone "in the hole."

In July, with Gordon still on death row, his female companion in the bank holdup received a seven-year sentence. Catherine Pilling, 23, the separated mother of two children, was dubbed the "Girl Bandit" in newspaper headlines. Judge Rey Sargent said she had no previous criminal record, but she had been an active participant in the bank raid and had driven the escape car. He told Pilling, "One of the men you associated with has a long record and at the present time is under sentence of death." Judge Sargent noted she had associated with other thugs in recent years, and although he didn't like sending women to prison, sex wouldn't alter his decision to impose a sentence "which will deter other foolish females from participating in armed robberies and holdups." She would be sent to the women's prison in Kingston, Ontario.

It probably didn't do too much for sales, but police reported that for the first time on record a small English-made car, a green Austin, was reported as the getaway car after a masked, armed man burst into a bank and escaped with money in yet another holdup.

It was that kind of summer in Vancouver as Gordon and Carey sweated it out on death row. Their lawyers worked on last-hope appeals, and the police reorganized and continued to battle the crooks still plaguing the city.

Jimmy Carey was banking on a successful appeal and sent an unusual letter to *The Vancouver Sun*, which was printed on September 7. From Oakalla he wrote:

> It has always been said that the English-speaking race are firm believers in "fair play." I am a man who has been convicted of murder, and from the court's point of view I had a fair trial. However I am being allowed an appeal, in which I have every hope of proving my innocence. The thing I find very hard to consider is "fair play" and the fact that while unlimited funds are available to the Crown to convict a man, only a very small and insignificant sum is allowed for the defence.[3]
>
> In my case—as I expect in most other murder

cases—friends and relatives ... even though they may be well off ... desert one. I suppose no one likes the stigma of a murder case, and my lawyer and I are under severe strain through lack of funds.

Is this fair—should I not have the right to as good a representation as the Crown to prove my case? I am writing to you asking if you or any of your readers know of any way I may raise sufficient funds for my defence.

Sincerely, James Carey

The *Sun* said B.C. allowed $150 for the defence, the "usual honorarium" for indigents charged with murder, in addition to lawyers' fees. Counsel Norman Mullins said he had $65 left after paying $75 for a copy of the transcript and a $10 phone call to Toronto. He said this was miniscule compared with the money and assets the Crown had at its disposal. Carey's parents were identified as a stepfather who was a banker in Toronto and his mother, who was a restaurateur. They obviously had taken the same view as Mrs. Gordon, that their son "had made his own bed, so let him lie in it." There was no money or moral support from them.

Public opinion on Carey's letter and plea was sharply divided. Most thought it was unmitigated gall on the part of a convicted murderer, while a minority considered it an argument with merit from a man convinced he could prove his innocence and save his life. There was, however, no great ground swell of discussion on the pros and cons of the situation and nothing at all from lawyers, other legal experts, or professors. Mervyn Davis of the John Howard Society was almost the lone commentator, stating that he was concerned about the inequity and would handle any money contributed in response to Carey's letter. The plea of a convicted killer didn't have the tug of campaigns for funds for orphans or injured animals. The *Sun* reported that a 60-year-old widow with a dying son had contributed $100 with money she had left over from mortgaging her house to pay bills, but she was the biggest donor. The last reported total of contributions to Carey's fund was $176.

Gordon and Carey's appeal opened in Victoria on September 19 before five judges of the B.C. Appeal Court. Trial prosecutor Bill Schultz contended there was no misdirection of the jury by Mr. Justice Manson. He pointed to the obvious: All but one of Gordon's defence witnesses were cons or ex-cons. Schultz described their court appearance as an "infamous parade of murderers, robbers, and thieves of every brand and variety."

Mullins argued that Carey had no intention of committing a crime on December 7 and that he had even taken his wife and child with him when he went out. He contended that his client was not charged with firing a shot in the incident and even claimed that Carey had taken the .45 revolver from the car before finally fleeing because he didn't want his wife to be found in the vehicle with it. The judges didn't seem impressed with Mullins' flight of fancy when he likened Carey to a partridge that flops away from the nest, feigning injury to distract the fox from its young. If anything they seemed to find Carey another kind of bird: too sly, too avaricious, and too fast on the wing. The appeal over, the judges said they would consider their decision.

In another odd and surprising move, Gordon and Carey preferred the cells of death row to those in which they were held in Victoria during the appeal. After the first day, they said they wanted to go back to Oakalla rather than face another night in the capital city's freezing jail. It was only September, but Carey said the draft had been so bad he slept on the floor rather than on his cot to try to avoid it. The strange request was allowed; they were escorted back to the mainland, while their lawyers soldiered on.

Mullins told the court that Manson had invited the jury to "reconstruct, to fabricate," evidence instead of setting out the defence fully and clearly. He added that only 12 of the 42 pages of the judge's charge dealt with his client. Hill was briefer. He said Gordon could not have been at the murder site because he had an alibi and witnesses. The lawyer contended that Manson "distorted" the evidence and didn't present the defence fully and adequately. He accused Manson of "twisting, misinterpreting, and erring."

During the appeal, there was another bank holdup in Vancouver that was much less than the perfect crime. The gunmen talked their way into jail. Three masked and armed men, again with a female getaway driver, got $8,626 in the robbery. When they returned to their east-end apartment. they were so pleased and elated that they discussed their holdup as they walked up to the front door. The fact that they were carrying a rifle added weight to their words. All of this was seen and heard by a man quietly gardening outside the building. He phoned police. When they raided the apartment, they arrested the four and recovered all the money, which was hidden in the kitchen oven, in the bathroom, and elsewhere in the rooms.

On September 26 there was bad news for Gordon from Victoria, relayed to him in Oakalla by Hill. The lawyer told him the judges had totally rejected his appeal and ruled that he must die. Hill held out only one last slim hope: consideration of an appeal to the Supreme Court of Canada.

Carey had reason to think he might be luckier. Mullins told him that the court had reserved judgment in his case and so a new trial was a possibility. Soon there was light at the end of Carey's dark tunnel. It was announced from Victoria that, by a 4–to–1 decision, the judges had agreed to grant him a new trial. Judge J.M. Coady said there had been "serious misdirection" by Manson and certain matters should have been left to the jury to decide. The dissenting judge, Sidney Smith, believed there was nothing wrong with Manson's charge. Prosecutor William Schultz immediately announced he would appeal the B.C. court's decision to the Supreme Court of Canada and oppose a new trial.

Meanwhile, in Ottawa, veteran Vancouver Island socialist MP Colin Cameron lashed out at the "savage sentences" being handed out in Vancouver and elsewhere in Canada, which he branded as the heaviest in the western world. Vancouver Police Chief George Archer, still trying to reorganize the force to fight the non-stop wave of crime he faced, disagreed and urged that sixteen-year-old offenders be charged in adult court, but his request was ignored.

In his continuing struggle to save Gordon from the hangman, and with the clock ticking away, Hill told the media in late October that he would appeal to federal Justice Minister Stuart Garson to grant clemency to the condemned man.

Amid all the stories of crime and violence and death sentences crowding newspaper pages, Vancouverites read one heartwarming case. It was a look back at another time and moral stance that for some had not changed with the passage of time. Mrs. Susan Gwyn had one of the few lucky breaks in her life. The ailing, 76-year-old pensioner won $4,420—more money than she had ever had before—in a radio contest. She told reporters that merchants on the prairies had allowed her credit during the Depression and she still had some outstanding bills. The first thing she planned to do with her newfound fortune was pay them off. Mrs. Gwyn hoped, however, that her much improved financial state wouldn't mean that the authorities would eject her and her sick 79-year-old husband from their pensioners' cottage in Burnaby. They didn't.

CAREY'S STORY

OFFICIAL CUSTODY INFLICTS IMAGINED TERROR AND FEAR. THE
FULL IMPACT IS LOST IN THE BITTERNESS IT BREEDS.

—*Excerpt from Joe Gordon's final message*

Christmas came and went with all the joy that could be expected in the cells on death row, where three others besides Gordon and Carey awaited execution. Because of the possibility of a new trial for Carey, the execution date for both him and Gordon was set back to February 12, and then to March 18. The wait went on, and as the new year of 1957 dawned, the drive to save the two men intensified, while the crime wave in Vancouver and around the province seemed to be unending.

For 31-year-old Richard Dowling of Duncan on Vancouver Island, the year didn't last long. The logger was shot dead following a row at a New Year's party in the early hours of January 1. He was B.C.'s first murder of the year. Later in the month, a bank robber attempted a holdup in Vancouver. The teller at the Royal Bank on West Hastings Street became aware that the man demanding money at her wicket was more than slightly drunk. She signalled to another staff member to call police, and while waiting for their arrival the tellers formed a circle around the would-be bandit. When police entered the bank, the happy hoodlum was leaning casually on the counter.

Many parents were concerned for their youngsters and looked everywhere to find reasons for any unusual behaviour. When the young disc jockey and teen favourite Red Robinson appeared at a usually staid Friday lunchtime dance at Lester Pearson High School, students went wild, screaming and gyrating to the beat. Principal Ian Taylor called off any future dances because of the bedlam. He indicated it was the behaviour and not the music that was the problem. He noted he had lived through the chicken scratch, turkey trot, lindy hop, black bottom, Lambeth walk, and bunny hug and wasn't about to get too excited about rock'n'roll. He said that if the music of Mozart or Beethoven produced such student reaction, he would rule it out as well.

As the days slipped into mid-February, the two men on death row faced a particularly bleak Valentine's Day. It was not a date Jimmy Carey remembered fondly. It was the date on which he had been arrested in Toronto the year before, and now on February 14 he learned that five of seven Supreme Court judges had ruled against the B.C. Appeal Court's decision recommending his new trial. It looked more and more like a last Valentine's Day for both men. Mullins announced that he would apply immediately to Ottawa for commutation of the death sentence. Carey's and Gordon's date with the executioner was now set for April 2, about seven weeks away.

On the calendar for execution before Gordon and Carey was death-row inmate E. Gordon Buck, aged 31. He had been convicted of the murder of his nine-year-old stepdaughter in Williams Lake. It was his second murder charge. He had been found not guilty of a similar charge in 1948 because of lack of evidence. Now he took his last walk, ashen and trembling. Like other condemned inmates, he too stated that he had found religion and was "at peace with God, with myself, and with my fellow man" just before he plunged down the shaft with a noose around his neck. For his last meal Buck had ordered a steak dinner and insisted that the four others on death row also be treated to one. The warden had the meals delivered to the cells of Gordon, Carey, and the two other men, but they went uneaten. No meal could be enjoyed on the day of a hanging. The four men sat waiting until once again they heard the terrible noise as the trapdoor slammed in the execution chamber.

Lawyer Norman Mullins decided to play one last card to save his client. It was played out on the pages of the *Vancouver Sun* on Thursday, February 21. A banner headline splashed across its front page read: "Death House Statement—James Carey Tells His Story of How City Policeman Slain." A subhead dramatized further: "One Chance Left to Miss Gallows." The story was by-lined James Carey.

Manson complained loudly that the story was an unprecedented interference with justice. He feigned puzzlement about how the paper got it, but it was almost certainly Mullins who provided the information. The story was given to *Sun* "sob sister" Simma Holt, but the published version had been brightly polished and bore the mark of one of the newspaper's stable of former purveyors of tear-jerking sensationalism in the English tabloids. A proviso stressed the paper wasn't endorsing the validity of Carey's claims, but was presenting them as one version of the case that had not previously been made public. The paper said only that this was a last desperate attempt to save Carey. In effect, the *Sun* offered the retrial evidence to the public that the court had refused to hear.

In consultation with his lawyers, Carey had originally decided not to enter the witness box to give evidence. It was now apparent that there had been a disagreement between Le Page and Mullins on this strategy. Since the trial Mullins had publicly represented Carey, and the accused now stated that a mistake had been made and he should have given his story to Manson and the jury. He feared the error would cost him his life. The *Sun's* front page carried large head-and-shoulders pictures of Carey and Gordon along with the long, long story. It was sensational and unprecedented in newspaper history in Canada at the time. The story was at times mawkish, dripping with self-pity, and hard to believe, but it sold newspapers by the dozens.

There's no doubt, however, that the widely read article and the publicity it generated became a pivotal factor in the next few days in the desperate campaign to save Carey's life. There was little or no hope for Gordon, who reportedly had pulled the trigger, but maybe there was a small chance for the man who walked with him on that dark December night.

The publicity generated when Jimmy Carey's story of the murder appeared in the Sun *was a pivotal factor in the campaign to save his life.*

Protesting his innocence, Carey began, "Now I know I should have taken the stand and would like to tell the story I'll never get a chance to tell to any jury." He wrote that he had long admired the police since they looked after him for a day when he got lost. He was eight years old at the time and visiting an aunt in Toronto, wearing a brand-new suit, and it was the first time he didn't have hand-me-downs. It's doubtful this part of the tale drew many tears, but Carey said he told it in order to explain why he helped police later when they asked him for criminal-investigation assistance. He wrote, "I went out on the street and was strutting around, showing off this suit, and somehow I got lost. The police picked me up and they drove me around in a police car, bought me candy and ice cream, and acted as though they really liked me. It was the happiest day of my life—next to the birth of my own baby, Lesley, in October 1955. It seems ironic that I should now be charged with the murder of a policeman."

Carey claimed this childhood experience was one of the reasons why he had had a long connection with the RCMP as an informant and had been willing to help them when they asked for his assistance. He kept his ears open and often picked up useful bits of underworld gossip. He claimed that in the summer of 1954 he heard of an initiative from the big boys in the drug trade. "I was told that $5,000 plus future benefits in the drug trade were being offered to anyone who would murder Danny Brent. I was told then that Danny's death would give the handlers of drugs full control of the street trade." Carey said he had warned Brent he was a target even though it failed to save the minor-league trafficker from the powerful drug gangs or prevent his own death on the golf-course fairway. As well, Carey talked to RCMP Constable Ed Carter. He wrote, "The Mounties advised me to carry on my associations within the drug trade and to keep them informed. I don't think Carter's superiors took much stock in what I told him."

Carey claimed he began to worry about getting too involved in the drug wars and decided to get out of his role with the RCMP by moving with Noreen to Invermere in the B.C. Interior, where he took a job in the mines there. About a month later, Carey said, he read about Brent's murder and heard that police were looking for someone matching his description. Carey claimed he called Bud Collier of the RCMP, a man he had known for some time who by then was serving with the detachment at Port Hardy on Vancouver Island. He did not explain how he knew this officer. Carey maintained that three days later, Collier contacted him and told him he had received a telegram from the RCMP commanding officer in Nelson, asking Carey to return to Vancouver to help in the Brent investigation. Nelson was the RCMP station serving Invermere. It wasn't explained why the top officer at this detachment would be involved, but Carey wrote that the message seemed to him to be almost an order. He was given expense money by a Corporal Payne and returned to Vancouver with Noreen. Upon his return he met with Carter and Sergeant Harold Price in a restaurant at Fourth Avenue and Alma on the city's west side and from then on worked under RCMP instructions as an informant.

"In order to be of aid to the police, I had to get deep into the underworld and occasionally had to participate in a crime in order not to arouse suspicion," Carey wrote. "Sergeant Price told me: 'It's a two-way street. You can probably make a few dollars but be careful of city police, particularly Rex Cray and Gus McDonald.' During the summer and fall I worked my way solidly into Vancouver's underworld."

Carey wrote that coming back from Invermere to the coast to try to help solve the Danny Brent murder was "the road to the gallows for me." He fingered Gordon for his plight, writing that if the police had not told him to stay close to Gordon, he would not have been with him at Watkins Winram. "I told them Joe was erratic and it was only a matter of time before he killed someone."

Carey claimed he had also worked on the Bill Semenick case. He stated that Noreen didn't know what he was doing and worried that he was becoming involved with gangsters. He wrote that he tried to break away and get another job but lost it when he couldn't be bonded because of his record. He was vague about the details of his arrests, admitting only that he was no angel and had been in trouble with the police, but never anything involving violence.

Carey said he was employed for a time with Bob Smith, who also hired Gordon as a salesman. Through this connection Gordon and the others started coming to his apartment, and because of his undercover work, he couldn't tell them not to do so. Carey asserted that he had turned down an offer from Gordon to join him and a woman in a bank holdup. He said he had located a .45 possibly used to kill Danny Brent that was now in Gordon's possession. He gave it to Carter, who returned it after tests showed it wasn't the gun that killed Brent.

Carey said Carter showed him the misshapen bullet that was fired and tested by police ballistics experts, commenting, "It's sure a mean-looking thing and would tear an awful hole in a man." I replied, "Well it's a cinch something like that will happen if he [Joe] gets in a bad spot." Carey said he took the gun home, not knowing for sure who actually owned it, Gordon or Stromson, but believing it was Gordon's. He later saw Stromson on the street and asked him to pick up the weapon, but Stromson said he would send Gordon to get it. He didn't; Carey still had the gun.

If even the slightest fraction of what Carey claimed to be his undercover work for the Mounties was true, it is inexplicable why his lawyers did not use it, and why his defence team didn't cross-examine Corporal Nick Carter at length when he testified at the trial.

Carey's story of the events of December 7, which appeared in its entirety in the *Sun*, began with Gordon's visit to his rented basement apartment in the east end. He claimed that when they left he was under the impression that Gordon was driving to a friend's house in Burnaby, where he and Noreen had a dinner date. He said this was why they took the baby with them. Smith later joined them and was given the .45, which he put under the car seat.

After driving in what seemed like the wrong direction, Carey said, he told Gordon that if he wasn't going to Burnaby they would get out and take a bus, but Gordon told him it was only a slight diversion. At the plant, according to Carey, Gordon and Smith got out, walked some distance, and then came back. "Gordon returned and said he was going to take another look. I got out of the car then to see where Joe was going. If he planned a robbery I'd know what the plans were and could tell Nick Carter," he explained.

Carey's version of how Sinclair was gunned down with two shots was graphic. "We walked around onto Third Avenue and there saw the police car drive up and stop. The officer called out, 'Come here you two.' I started towards him. I had no gun on me—nothing incriminating—so I had nothing to fear. Then suddenly Joe pulled out a gun. I yelled, 'For God's sake, Joe. Don't be crazy. Put that away.' For a split second I thought of trying to argue with Joe, but I was unarmed and knew if I fought with Joe he might use the gun on me. I did the only thing possible for me. I turned and ran. I heard Joe say, 'All right just a minute.' I ran down Granville and was at Fourth and Granville—about a block away—when I heard two shots. For a second I thought Joe was shooting at me. I ran for the car and jumped in. As the car was moving Joe jumped in and Smith drove off."

Carey repeated his wife's warning of a following police car. "Joe Gordon was hysterical. He screamed, 'I shot the guy. Let me out.'" Carey said he got out after Gordon and took the .45 out of the car and threw it away. At this point in the narrative the prose and style of Carey's story mirrored the tabloids at their best. "Oh, God, I whispered a prayer, don't let police fire at the car and hurt the two inside [Noreen and baby]." Carey said he ran, confirming also that he was the one that the young witness Peters saw rushing in the front door and out the back of a nearby rooming house in his bid to escape the pursuing cop. He claimed he hid under the porch of a nearby house through the long, wet night. Carey wrote that he learned of the murder when he heard a news report of Sinclair's slaying from a radio in a room above his hiding place. "I was sick," Carey wrote.

The next day he made his way to where Noreen and the baby were staying. When he saw them, he suddenly thought of the slain policeman's family: "I thought of Mrs. Sinclair who may have a baby and I just broke down and wept. I think about Mrs. Sinclair often and worry about how she is doing. I want her to know that I didn't have anything to do with killing her husband. I wrote her a letter sometime in August and gave it to a friend. Maybe sometime that friend will get it to her."

He said it was then that Noreen told him that while he was out of the apartment she had helped make a mask for Gordon. "Judge Manson referred to the tall man wearing a mask. I never saw Gordon or Smith with a mask. I didn't have one," Carey wrote, although an eyewitness saw a man wearing one, and the mask exhibited at the trial was found at the scene. He said that in a brief visit to the apartment he found part of the old underwear that had been used to make the mask. He collected the pieces and burned them in the furnace.

His story contended that when Noreen asked him what happened at Watkins Winram, he told her, "Noreen you know as much as I do about it. I ran away when I saw a police car and for all I know from the time Joe made the statement and I hid under the house it could have been the policeman shooting or Gordon. He's crazy. I thought for several seconds he was shooting at me."

Carey claimed he had later talked to Carter on the phone. Carter said he knew how Carey felt about Lamont and McCullough being on the case and said he had been trying to contact Detective Bill Morphett, the city policeman working with the RCMP on the Brent murder. Carey wrote that Carter then advised him: "Give yourself up and phone me back at one o'clock. Where are Noreen and Lesley?" But Carey said he didn't phone back and finally decided to flee Vancouver at the urging of Noreen and the friends at whose home she was staying. He left on a bus for eastern Canada.

His story pressed the pathos button: "Going out the door, when I kissed Noreen goodbye, I remember saying, 'I think I'm doing wrong. I should phone Nick again.' However, it's easy to see I did not. I ran again. I guess I was terribly confused and easily persuaded. On that bus trip there wasn't a moment that my thoughts weren't on those two I loved so much. It is hard to explain what a man who has never had a family to call his own in his life feels when he has his very own baby and wife. Just to think I'll never see little Lesley again."

Carey wrote that he soon recognized his fleeing was a mistake. "I realized it wouldn't matter if I was one block or one mile away when the shots were fired if I was in cahoots with Gordon, but I had no plan whatsoever with him. If I planned a robbery, I certainly would not endanger the life of my child by taking her along. I can't say why Gordon killed Mr. Sinclair because I didn't see it happen. I only know what he told me."

The most perplexing point, perhaps, was his work for the RCMP. He wrote, "I knew if Carter told the whole story I would be okay, but my lawyer at that time (Le Page) hardly cross-examined him because he said there was nothing against me." Carey explained his role simply: "I got mixed advice about what to do."

His story concluded: "If I knew then what I know now, I wouldn't be on Death Row looking at that terrible door behind which the gallows is set up. I can still hear the crack of the trap door from the night Graham was hanged and still feel sick from Tuesday's hanging of Buck. Oh, God help me. I cannot help myself."

There are several sequences in Carey's story that are hard to believe. After hearing Sinclair calling them and seeing Gordon pull a gun, Carey said he had time to run a block before hearing the shots. If he was already a block away, it would be unlikely that the shots were aimed at him. All the previous evidence pointed to only split seconds between Sinclair pulling up at the scene and his being killed. It was also clear that Sinclair was shot in the face as soon as he started to get out of the patrol car, because one of his legs was still inside the vehicle when his body was found.

Carey said it was all a grievous error from the start: being with Gordon, running from the scene, taking poor advice, leaving B.C., working for the RCMP, and not testifying on his own behalf because his counsel told him there was no evidence against him.

Some people thought Carey's story was an outrageous lie cooked up by a convicted murderer to try to stir up public sympathy and escape the hangman. But while much of the story could be a combination of lies and fantasy, there was enough truth to suggest that Carey had been involved quite deeply with the Mounties in undercover work. Why then wasn't Carter cross-examined by Le Page at the trial? Some speculated that this didn't happen because Carey's story was all fiction, concocted after the jury found him guilty. Somewhere, however, there seemed to be a kernel of truth, and there was too much detail for it to be totally untrue. Did the Mounties in fact pay him? He claimed there was correspondence regarding his work for the RCMP, but where was it? Not only Carter, but also the other policemen named *could* have been questioned and were not. A new trial would have provided an answer, but the Supreme Court of Canada had disallowed the B.C. Appeal Court's decision.

LAWYERS' DISAGREEMENT

THE ARCHAIC AND MEDIEVAL STATUTES PROTECTING SOCIETY ARE REPREHENSIBLE. THE QUESTION OF TODAY IS: WHO SHALL PROTECT A DELINQUENT OR FOR THAT MATTER A CRIMINAL FROM SOCIETY?

—Excerpt from Joe Gordon's final message

The newspaper publication of Carey's story sparked new petitions for a new trial for him. The federal government had the power to order one in spite of the Supreme Court ruling. The man behind the last-minute drive to try to save Carey's life was Mullins, who told reporters he would talk to any group, any time, any place, to try to drum up support. Mullins said Carey deserved another trial because he would not have been involved but for his undercover work for the Mounties. Bad decisions had induced him not to testify. Mullins made it clear that there had been a split in the defence team, pointing out that he had only been the junior counsel, and the decision to keep Carey from testifying in his own defence came entirely from Le Page.

There was no great ground swell of support, however. Very few people rushed to sign the petition, but there remained an uneasy feeling that disclosures in Carey's story supported granting him a new trial. The underworld didn't agree. In its view, Carey was a stoolie, a police informant, who should get what he deserved in the old elevator chute at Oakalla.

Mullins asked Ottawa for an official report on Carey's claims of undercover work. He also sent a message to American detective-story author Erle Stanley Gardner who ran a "Court of Last Resort" that looked into controversial cases. It had a small record of helping some accused receive a measure of justice through publicity. These news stories didn't hurt Gardner's book sales, either. In the House of Commons, Vancouver CCF Member of Parliament Harold Winch asked Justice Minister Stuart Garson if he had read Carey's story in the *Sun* and his RCMP claims. The minister said no, but he would.

By March 7, with less than two weeks until Carey's scheduled date with the hangman, the *Sun* reported that interest in the accused's plight had picked up and that it had received almost 2,000 letters urging a new trial. The paper also disclosed that the remissions branch of the federal justice department was studying the new issues raised by the story and would report to Solicitor General Ross MacDonald. He would relay the findings to cabinet, which could order a new appearance for Carey if it chose. Winch had a two-hour meeting with Garson, pressing the issue, but told newsmen there was no change of heart from the government.

Mullins dashed off a wire to the minister, stating, "I am amazed in a case where the life of a man is at stake that you made a decision against retrial without waiting for counsel's brief." Mullins had just airmailed an eight-page letter to Garson. The lawyer also charged that Schultz had withheld information about Carey's undercover role, resulting in a "very grave miscarriage of justice."

In an unusual twist, Hill appeared before Justice Manson, seeking a reprieve for Gordon. He presented a strange note, which he said Carey had given to Gordon just before they went to Victoria for their appeal hearing. According to the lawyer, it was a small, soiled piece of paper that Gordon had given to someone at Oakalla for safekeeping, and it had just come into his possession. It was unsigned, and it didn't make much sense. Carey was purported to have written, "Could I do any good when the rabbi comes to talk if I would tell the truth and clear you and single me out as the one—and lead up to him having a discussion with me." It flew in the face of Carey's every effort to finger Gordon and exculpate himself.

Manson, as expected, was highly sceptical, dismissing the note and turning down the bid for a reprieve. The judge said every opportunity had been given the accused, but he still had been convicted and his appeals rejected by the courts. An annoyed Manson then took a swing at Mullins and at the newspaper campaign launched by the *Sun*. "Of course any admission would be entirely inconsistent with a most unfortunate campaign that has been carried on by the *Vancouver Sun* for some weeks and such a campaign as has never before been conducted by any newspaper in Canada. It is unfortunate in that it may mislead some people who were not present at the trial and don't know the evidence," complained the judge.

The people, of course, had followed all the extensive stories carried by the papers, television, and radio, but Manson dismissed them all. With a good idea of how the paper got Carey's story, Manson nevertheless feigned bewilderment, saying that no permission had been granted for any reporters to talk to the condemned man. Of course, Mullins had talked to him many times as his defence lawyer.

The judge said the statements made by Carey could not be reconciled with the contents of the mystery note produced by Hill, but he went out of his way to praise Hill and indirectly slam Mullins. He said Gordon's lawyer had not attempted to have the case tried in the press, which "has not helped any of us and is a discredit to our judicial procedures." He added, "Mr. Hill is perhaps late but it is never too late when a man's life is at stake." If it was indicated, Manson added, that Garson was prepared to consider the new material presented by Hill, he would accede to the reprieve motion. "Not for a moment would I reject this application if the minister thinks there is sufficient merit in this representation made to him to necessitate a reprieve, but I can not grant it on the material as it stands before me," added the judge.

On March 15 Mullins received a letter from Garson, dated the eleventh, stating that Carey's fate was still in the balance. The minister said that contrary to press reports, no decision had been made on a new trial prior to his receiving the lawyer's eighteen-page submission. The clock ticked on.

Just before March 18, as tension mounted at Oakalla and everyone braced themselves for back-to-back hangings, there was a last-minute call from Ottawa. Garson asked Schultz to get a delay while senior justice officials flew to Vancouver to try to sort out what if any meaning there was in the alleged note that Hill had presented. No one knew what to think of this latest development in the life-or-death drama.

On death row, Gordon and Carey were told that they had been spared temporarily. Manson set a new execution date of April 2, postponing the hangings for another two weeks. With the gallows ready and the executioner waiting, Warden Hugh Christie put all arrangements on hold. The pair had already written their last letters and seen their last visitors. A rabbi had visited Gordon. The *Sun* quoted an unidentified spokesman as stating that for the first time since he had been arrested on the murder charge more than fourteen months earlier, Gordon was ready to die. Carey wasn't.

No mention was made publicly, but it could be assumed that many questions were being asked in Ottawa concerning Carey's allegations that he had been involved with the RCMP; senior police officers were probably still being asked if there was any truth to his claim of having worked undercover. Even if he had, it had no direct bearing on the murder of Gordon Sinclair. It could only carry weight in the argument that Carey should be imprisoned rather than hanged.

The public also learned from frank new police chief Archer that every recent move made to combat the ever-increasing crime wave had been unsuccessful. January and February 1957 had been the worst in Vancouver's history. There had been 93 robberies with violence, and bandits had hit 34 small grocery stores. More police, more patrol cars, and a special commando squad "didn't help," confessed Archer. He said that while new methods would be tried, more help was needed from the public. The only good news was that more crooks had been caught. There were suggestions from the public for more reward money and an alarm system for stores. Archer quickly rejected public reaction that called for a vigilante force to help cops fight crime and that suggested store operators be armed.

With another fourteen days before the next execution date, Mullins declared, "We'll all be sweating it out again but we have time to work on it now." Attorney General Bonner rejected a request by Erle Stanley Gardner's group to conduct a lie-detector test. Bonner sniffed and said this process and the machine had no place in B.C.'s judicial system.

The press continued to badger the police and lawyers for information as the fourteen precious days for Gordon and Carey wore on. Nobody was saying much. A.J. McLeod, the director of the remissions branch, had flown to Vancouver from Ottawa. Ostensibly, he had been sent to probe the mystery note that Carey was supposed to have passed to Gordon and which had been rejected by Manson when Hill produced it in court. He was, however, actually looking into the claims about Carey's undercover work for the RCMP. McLeod would only say to reporters that he had interviewed both men and their lawyers and questioned them closely. He spent long hours talking to Gordon and Carey in their cells. The defence lawyers spelled out for the media the options: execution of both convicted men, a slim chance that Carey might get a new trial ordered by cabinet, and finally, commutation by the federal government of both death sentences.

The news that arrived from Ottawa 48 hours before the execution date didn't involve the pair on death row. It was announced that RCMP hero Bud Johnstone had been awarded the George Medal for gallantry in the bank gun battle that took the life of Herbert Howerton. At quiet Qualicum Beach on Vancouver Island, where he now headed the two-man detachment, Johnstone would only allow that he felt a "little excited" about the news of the award. He added that he found his new job "nice and quiet."

The end of March came and went. There was only silence from Ottawa. Warden Christie had the execution arrangements restored at Oakalla, where the hangman was waiting. Tension mounted at the jail over the impending hanging. This was a grimmer situation than most, as it was to be a double hanging, and one had not been performed in many years.

NO MERCY FOR JOE

"YOU BREAK LAWS ... THE PRICE: YOUR LIFE."

—Excerpt from Joe Gordon's final message

April 1 dawned a beautiful, sunny, spring day. The executions were scheduled for a few minutes after midnight; at least Gordon and Carey wouldn't die on April Fools' Day. At 9:45 a.m. a ringing phone shattered the grim silence in Warden Christie's office. The federal cabinet had made their decision: Carey's life would be spared, but there was to be no mercy for Joe Gordon. He would die.

Carey was quickly moved from his death-row cell to another part of the jail. Mullins told reporters that Carey had commented, "I had the feeling something new would turn up." The three letters he had written to his child, to be given to her at certain birthdays, could now be thrown away.

Mullins cautioned that Carey could still lose his life. There was the possibility that other convicts could act to avenge Gordon, whom they felt had been betrayed by his partner in crime, a man now exposed as a secret police informer. The lawyer said he was scared for his client but felt Carey could look after himself, although he was in a very tough league. Mullins stressed that he would press to have Carey moved to a penitentiary outside B.C., but jail scuttlebutt moved quickly through prisons across Canada and many people felt the move wouldn't mean a thing if somebody really was out to get him. As soon as he was moved off death row, he was placed under special protection, but officials knew he couldn't be protected forever.

The underworld despised Carey. An unidentified Oakalla guard told the *Sun*, "If Gordon hangs, the convicts will feel Carey has saved his own life over Gordon's dead body. Any long-time convict would be quite happy to slit his throat."

The cabinet decision was relayed to Manson, who immediately wired Ottawa, calling in "the strongest possible terms" for similar mercy for Gordon. He still thought both of them were murderers who had been fairly and justly treated by the legal process, but if one was to be saved from the gallows so should the other. The John Howard Society made a similar plea, but to no avail.

Noreen Carey got the news at home. She happily told reporters, "Wherever he is Jimmy will be the only man for me. I will be with him every visitor's day and take our daughter along." After narrowly missing the noose, Carey was already said to be arrogantly demanding that Mullins work to get him as short a prison sentence as possible. He still faced life. There was no comment from Gordon's family.

Learning that his partner in crime had escaped the fate he now faced, Gordon's anger at Carey boiled over. He scribbled his feelings in some of the last notes he wrote. He sent one to Mullins, and three to other convicts he knew. Reporters were told that Gordon's notes conveyed a warning to the trio of friends that they could wind up condemned like him. One was for the brother of Mac Ramsay, Rod, who was the youngest of the four Ramsay boys. He took Gordon's words to heart; he got a job with the railway, married, and had a family before he retired as yardmaster. He said all his brothers worked in the shipyards when they left home, and "it was a breeding ground for crime." Gordon's fifth letter was for the public.

Rabbi Bernard Goldenberg visited Gordon on death row, but after a short stay Gordon asked him to leave. He also told the rabbi not to attend the hanging. Goldenberg complied with Gordon's wishes, but he did make one last attempt to help him. He contacted a friend, lawyer Arthur Fouks, to ask if anything more could be done for Gordon. Fouks in turn got in touch with well-known criminal defender Angelo Branca, and the two lawyers rushed to the penitentiary that night for one last meeting with Warden Christie.

On April 1, 1957, Jimmy Carey escaped the fate that awaited his partner in crime, Joe Gordon.

But they could do nothing to stay the execution. Gordon turned down the chance of a special last meal.

With only a few hours left for Joe, Reverend Stanley Higgs, president of the Vancouver Council of Churches, made the last appeal to Ottawa. Opponents of capital punishment made many calls to Oakalla, pushing for mercy in the final hours of Gordon's life. Prison authorities could do nothing more, and the only hope for the condemned man was a last-minute phone call conveying Ottawa's change of heart. Midnight came. Warden Christie did as he had promised and waited five minutes, but the phone did not ring; the clock moved on, and the die was cast.

At 12:13 a.m. on April 2, 1957, Joe Gordon took the short walk from his cell to the execution chamber. He had refused medication and was ashen-faced but calm. He was thinner than he had been fifteen months earlier. The silent chamber was crowded with observers: six members of the coroner's jury; the sheriff; four media representatives; and other prison staff, including six guards who stood with their backs to the executioner. Without assistance Joe Gordon moved onto the platform, setting his feet firmly at the centre, and then he looked at his audience. He seemed unafraid, self-assured, cocky, and arrogant to the end.

A sneer passed over his face before Camille Branchaud, the hangman, stepped behind him and slipped a black silk hood over his head. Then the noose, a one-inch-thick yellow rope, was slipped into place. The hangman hit the lever, and Joe Gordon plunged down the old elevator shaft to his death. The rope swung back and forth as the witnesses were asked to leave the execution chamber. It had been only about one minute since Joe Gordon entered the room. The 34-year life of the bank-holdup man, car thief, robber, drug user, and cop killer was over. He became the third-to-last man put to death by the justice system in B.C., the nineteenth-to-last in all of Canada. Manson's "big, bad wolf" and the underworld's charismatic, swaggering, slick, streetwise man of the moment was no more.

The prison doctor pronounced him dead at 12:25 a.m., twelve minutes after the crash of the trapdoor had echoed throughout Oakalla. Jimmy Carey heard the sound loud and clear and undoubtedly cringed in his cell. The hatred Joe Gordon had held for him at the end was vividly expressed in the note he left for Carey's lawyer, which was made public after his execution. Gordon wrote in spidery handwriting:

> To Mr. Mullins;
> It is traditional for a condemned person to say a few last words. I am no different from others before me in as much as facing the facts are concerned. Ere I depart this world of hypocrisy, to the general

public I make these observations: I have yet to meet a stool pigeon who would not sell his miserable soul for a phony three-dollar bill. This case has proved that. To Mr. Hill and Rabbi Goldenberg, I express my deep appreciation for their sincere belief in me and for their many kindnesses. May all my friends remember me for what I am, not for what others with their libelous remarks, make me out to be. Some day the world at large will acknowledge my innocence, of that I am sure.

Thanks, Joe Gordon.

JOE'S FINAL MESSAGE

IN RETROSPECT THE PHRASE "BORN TO DIE" LEAPS INTO MIND.
AS SOPHOCLES PUT IT: "NEVER TO HAVE BEEN BORN
IS MUCH THE BEST, AND THE NEXT BEST BY FAR,
TO RETURN WHENCE BY THE WAY SPEEDIEST,
WHERE OUR BEGINNINGS ARE."

—Excerpt from Joe Gordon's final message

The world at large did its best to forget Joe Gordon, although the Sinclairs would always remember the man who killed their husband and father. Apart from his friends in the underworld, there was little doubt in the public mind that Joe Gordon was a murderer who deserved to die. Hanging still had the support of a large majority in the country in the mid-1950s. What his family thought was never stated publicly, but despite his mother's attitude and her statement that he was no longer a member of the family, one of his sisters quietly claimed his body. She made sure that Joe Gordon was buried outside the prison grounds.

The public, however, learned much more about Joe Gordon after his death than they had known during his lifetime. Always one to make a grandstand play, Gordon wrote a long essay during his final few days in prison. It was essentially a warning to parents to be kinder and more loving with their children because, he said, rough, uncaring, and violent treatment from his father had started him on the road that led to death row. It was a powerful message that even now, nearly 50 years after it was written, is worth consideration.

It ran on the *Sun's* front page the day of his execution, by-lined Joe Gordon and entitled "Born To Die." It pushed the account and the details of the hanging to an inside page and it was printed exactly as he wrote it.

Whatever good I can do before I depart this world of pain and tears, let me do now ... so that whatever joy and happiness I may bring can in some measure replace the sufferings that others may feel. Juvenile delinquency begins in the home, and expands on the street, for the path of juvenile delinquency is but a step from the road of crime and that twisting, tortuous lane of unfortunate humans who walk by night; the lepers of society. For some it is a means of experience; for others a career. Live dangerously and die young—to use a tired cliché.

As one glances in retrospect the phrase "born to die" leaps into mind. As Sophocles put it:

"Never to have been born is much the best,
And the next best by far,
To return whence by the way speediest,
Where our beginnings are."

Every person has criminal elements within him—but he is not born a criminal. Many factors go into the ruination of a personality; home environment and parental love are basic in the development of a child.

I was born in Montreal. There I had my first taste of bitterness, sorrow and pain. Mine was a heart yearning for the love I felt was denied by my father.

You are raised in a large family—a middle-class home which includes four sisters and three other brothers. But somehow you are unlike them. You receive practically the same sort of treatment by your parents as the others, but you feel something is lacking. You think you are not receiving the love and understanding you think you deserve.

Then again, it is probably the resentment every time you receive a severe thrashing from your father. You believe your father indulges the whims of your brothers and sisters, but you are scolded or receive the strap.

Perhaps because you seem more mature, you are left to your own devices and consequently, not having reached the age of reason, emotions rule. You feel unwanted. Bewildered, just beginning public school, you come to know the gnawing sensation of hatred. Anxiety and pain, humiliation and sorrow in those tender years become a scar seared in your soul. It will grow larger with age.

In 1929 my family moved to Vancouver. I was six when I first entered the juvenile detention home—my crime—running away from home. My punishment—the strap, the reason I ran away in the first place. That first night in the detention home was a terrible one. Thrust among older boys than myself—all complete strangers—led to my first step into crime.

Instead of a kindly father to son chat, I received the treatment I had come to fear. Fear is a strange emotion. You may cringe from pain, but despite this respect is lacking. In its place bitterness and rebellion is born. Respect and understanding can never be won by parents through fear of physical pain. It builds resentment for all authority. No one was interested in your reactions, only your obedience.

The fundamental principle of life is self preservation. You blindly follow instinct and fight with whatever means at your command. Unfortunately, the only weapons at your disposal are those not controlled by authority. Willful desire and thoughtless emotion rule. Consequently, you break laws regardless of personal sacrifice and loss. The price you pay can never be repaid. The price: Your life.

As a child, as an adolescent, and more recently as an adult, I sought a substitute for the heart-rending path that only the lonely know. You haven't reached the age when you are able to reason the "whys" and "wherefores." You follow where emotions and instinct lead. You are guided by frustration, hate and the compulsion of those emotions.

In his book Protecting Children from a Criminal Career, J.R. Ellington writes: "All talk of a loving God or of loving one's neighbour will carry no meaning to a child who has not himself felt the warm love of parents. Little respect for others can be expected from one whose childhood experiences have not built up in him, respect for himself."

At the age of 12 I was sent to the Boys Industrial School. It was far different from what I understand it is today. I was sentenced to the Industrial School three times for petty offences. Each time I learned more of crime. Punishment succeeds very well in making criminals. It also keeps you on the road of crime and in the company of criminals. Those poor unfortunates who were to be my friends welcomed me. Why not? Misery loves company. Also the most compassionate people are criminals for they have suffered the rejection of society.

You learn from them how to steal a car, break into any sort of dwelling, blow open a safe, how to become a drug addict, a drug connection and a gun man. You become brutal at times, bitter always. You are also soft and sentimental—championing the underdog. You are not yet 15 when sentenced first to Oakalla Prison farm, for possession of burglary tools. In prison I learned what a drug addict was. I was given my first taste of drugs at Oakalla.

Prison taught me what I know and is teaching others. The only friends I have in life are criminals. Due process of law brought me into contact with them in the first instance.

Where no one else I had met showed any interest in my behaviour, these criminals showed me friendship and understanding which I eagerly accepted. Drug addicts, gunmen, pimps and prostitutes—those denizens of the underworld cast out by society—proved to be more humane than their socially acceptable counterparts.

No one is entirely good or entirely bad. We all excuse our own failures but seldom, if ever, do we excuse the failures of others. The archaic and medieval statutes protecting society are reprehensible. The question of today is: Who shall protect a delinquent or for that matter, a criminal from society?

Every child should be considered sacred and all children equal in this sanctity. Remember, indirectly we taught our children to be delinquents but failed to teach them the meaning of the word. As a voice in the wilderness crying for aid, teenagers plead for help, but there is none to lend a helping hand. No lifeline is thrown; no assurance or comfort given. It is survival of the fittest and self preservation first. Oscar Wilde wrote: "The easiest way to resist temptation is to yield."

Can we blame immature kids for falling prey to temptation? If adults can not resist, how can we expect adolescents to do otherwise? Instead of breaking a kid's heart why not give him a break and help him. Don't wait while irreparable damage is done to their growing personality traits. To brand a delinquent a criminal is to all but abandon hope.

There is probably no longer or lonelier night in the lifetime of a child than the first one spent in a detention home. Official *custody inflicts imaginary terror and fear. The full impact is lost in the bitterness it breeds.*

Sending youngsters to prison puts them in a school of criminal knowledge. Those who were not criminals when they entered will be so on their discharge. Instead of correcting young offenders, it more often demoralizes and hardens them.

The public servants aren't interested in guilt or innocence; their sole interest lies in conviction. They condemn 10 when one is guilty—and feel themselves justified. Their power is frightening when you realize they are instrumental in shaping the future of so many youngsters. They rely on the time-worn phrase, "society must be protected." Juveniles must also be protected from those prone to condemn and convict without factual evidence. Emphasis should not be placed on cure alone but on prevention.

Social workers and criminologists—although sincere in their desire to help—all too often fail when most needed. No doubt the majority of trained scientists today were themselves juvenile delinquents in their youth. In their day, however, their acts were called childish pranks, normal actions of youngsters.

This is not a tirade against society. It is meant as a frank appraisal of what society should be and how it can protect its future. The youngster of today will represent society of tomorrow.

Guided by understanding and parental love, these juveniles may well be tomorrow's leaders and go on to help other good citizens.

Written laboriously in his spidery handwriting, this message from a death cell was Joe Gordon's legacy, all that was left from a violent, wasted life. Whether his words were all true or whether they were what he wanted to remember is not known. When his mother disowned him, talking to a reporter shortly after Gordon was sentenced to die, she insisted that her son left the family. She was probably right. It was likely, however, that the reasons he gave for leaving were valid.

Joe Gordon's final words were soon forgotten, despite the fact that in Vancouver, even in all of B.C., there had never been a last message like his from a condemned killer. Believable or not, he made his points, his arguments, suggestions, and pleas. His letter might have been the basis of study and comment by those interested and working in the fields of delinquency and the social sciences; perhaps it did influence some of them, but that is unknown.

In more recent times, social workers and psychologists have recognized that an abusive childhood can destroy anyone. In Gordon's time, Victorian principles of instant obedience tended to predominate, particularly in any family exposed to military discipline. Imposing that criterion and combining it with denied affection and physical or emotional abuse is as destructive today as it was then. It remains one of the evils of our time, but at least it is now recognized as a problem. In Gordon's day it wasn't. There are now foster care homes, women's and children's care facilities, community-based services for children and teens, family justice programs, and a host of other government-funded initiatives whereby trained personnel do their best to deal with the complicated problems of today's ethnically diverse and quickly changing society. There is no question that the Canadian environment today imposes stress on many families, particularly the children. Unfortunately, as in Gordon's time, the social and legal system too often seems to fail.

Juvenile detention homes no longer function as schools for young criminals, but their role has been usurped by teen gangs, which in some locations teach all the tricks of the trade to a growing number of teens who are torn between obeying their parents and becoming one of the gang at school. Absentee parents, or those who speak no English, pose another problem, as they leave their teenaged youngsters open to threats of violence, bribery, and even death from those gangs who delight in the power they wield over their peers.

Gordon's letter to the public called for loving parents and a more just society. Canada has moved a long way toward agreeing with his reasoning; however, in the 21st century it is just as difficult as it was in the 1950s to ensure that youngsters are loved enough and protected in the home.

POST-MORTEM

J oe Gordon had been dead for only hours when news about the allocation of the $6,000 in reward money came to public attention. A panel consisting of Alderman Jack Cornett, Police Commissioner Cecil Merritt, and city solicitor Rhodes Elliott had made the decision and later presented their recommendations to city council for approval. Surprising to many people was the fact that the man who got the gun for Gordon and later told police where to find it received one third of the total amount—$2,000. James Miller was the petty crook and dope addict who testified during the trial that he was delayed in informing police about the location of the weapon because he was shooting up dope and that was more important than anything else in his world. He had cut a deal with police: in exchange for the opportunity to dodge charges pending against him, he had agreed to provide evidence during the trial. The $2,000 award also put Miller at the top of the list as a prime candidate for the gangland justice that would be meted out by Gordon's many friends. Miller, very wisely, immediately left town and headed for eastern Canada.

The Nielsens, the young immigrant couple who lived under the bridge near the Watkins Winram plant, also received a $2,000 reward, and the final third went to Betty Hood, the dry-cleaning company employee who had helped to destroy Gordon's alibi by testifying to the true times he had visited the store following Sinclair's murder. The panel dismissed four other claimants' bids for the money.

That same day, it was revealed by Gordon's lawyer that another letter had been written by the convicted murderer. This time Gordon claimed he was actually the man who had robbed a city drugstore, not John Graham Bryson, who had been convicted of the crime and was serving a six-year sentence. Bryson, aged 45, had a record going back 22 years and had been arrested and charged after Irma and Dave Brail were held up in their drugstore at 3175 Oak Street. The robbery occurred about five months before Sinclair was murdered. The owners were locked in a storeroom by a masked gunman, who later phoned police to tell them where to find the couple. Although the robber wore a mask, Mrs. Brail said she had identified him because of his sandy-coloured hair, his height (Bryson was taller than Gordon), and because he had a peculiar walk and a voice that she readily identified. She pointed out that Gordon's hair was short and curly. Authorities checked out Gordon's assertion, but it didn't help Bryson, who served his full term in jail.

Gordon left a will, the terms of which were never disclosed. Ironically, it was a lawyer visiting Oakalla, William Craig, an assistant city prosecutor who had appeared for the Crown during Gordon's appeal, who was asked to witness his signature on the document.

Jack Wasserman, the *Vancouver Sun* columnist whose lively and witty commentary was often the talk of the town, had some comments to make on the Gordon case. He covered the late-night celebrity beat and seldom ended his working day before the wee hours. He slept days. Because of his connections with performers, cabaret and club owners, and night-beat cops and his general knowledge of the downtown scene, he broke a number of stories, and his colourful contentions were often difficult to prove or disprove. When he sometimes took on duties as an amateur sleuth, he often discussed the options with fellow journalist and crime reporter Jack Webster. The day Joe Gordon was hung, Wasserman claimed that when Sinclair pulled up at the Watkins Winram plant, he called out, "Gordon, come here." The policeman supposedly was leaning back into his cruiser to get his radio mike when Gordon fired. Only days later, Wasserman contended that Gordon killed Sinclair because he "thought Sinclair was going to lunge at him as he got out of the car." Oakalla guards had heard Gordon confessing to other inmates that this was the reason he had fired the gun, the columnist claimed.

It was a typical Wasserman exposé, but this time the accounts seemed extremely fanciful. There were no witnesses at the scene and no one else had heard these conversations. All the evidence pointed to there being only split seconds between Sinclair's arrival at the scene and the gunfire that witnesses heard. Did Gordon say these things to fellow inmates? It seems highly questionable. Wasserman also maintained that while condemned men were given drugs just before their execution, Oakalla Prison authorities allowed Gordon to have them for several days before the date. Oakalla did not confirm or deny this assertion.

One of Wasserman's disclosures appears more probable than the others. It was obtained from employees of a downtown club, who told him that one of their customers, scant hours after Gordon went through the trapdoor, was the hangman. He was remembered, the columnist wrote, because he was "a one-dollar-tip man."

THE PIPER PLAYS ON

A Son Recalls

Ian Sinclair recalls watching and listening in the Supreme Court as the men who murdered his father were sentenced to death. He wasn't filled with hate for trigger man Joe Gordon or quietly gloating that he was to hang, he said nearly 50 years later. "I simply felt that after many sad and angry months justice had finally taken its course and the jury had reached a proper decision," he stated. Today, he would support a return of the death penalty for premeditated murder. He wasn't angered when Jimmy Carey escaped the noose: "He wasn't the one who actually pulled the trigger.

Sinclair credits the *Vancouver Sun* campaign and the minority but highly vocal anti-hanging advocates of the time with swaying the federal cabinet decision to grant Carey amnesty, pointing out that he spent about fifteen years in the penitentiary before being released. Then he fled to eastern Canada and moved on to the Maritimes, where he served more time for sex offences involving children. He now resides in New Brunswick. Noreen didn't wait for Carey, and he didn't look her up after he was released. Noreen remarried and continues to live in British Columbia, as does her daughter Lesley.

Time has blurred some of the events, but Sinclair said he never had any doubt that Gordon's appeals would be dismissed. He can't recall if he waited up until after midnight on April 2, 1957, to hear that the death penalty was carried out. The execution brought him no particular satisfaction. He remembers the months leading to it as a difficult time for all the children and for his mother, as it renewed their feelings of loss for their father and husband. Agnes Sinclair was distraught and kept the vow she made hours after her husband's death—that she would never remarry. The three teenagers were stunned without their much-loved father, who had been so brutally torn away from them. Too young to appreciate the danger their father's job entailed, they had been shocked by the sudden loss of the man at the centre of their lives. Money also was a problem for the family; the survivors' pension was small, but fortunately the publicly raised funds helped to bolster their income. Agnes Sinclair kept working, moving from Kitsilano High School to another pastry cook job at Churchill High.

Ian Sinclair, who now lives in retirement in Coquitlam, is the father of three children and grandfather of two. His sisters both live in B.C. and are married with children. His mother is in her 80s.

Although he was to be a policeman for 36 years, Ian Sinclair wasn't immediately motivated to follow in his father's footsteps. He didn't rush into the job as soon as he was old enough from a spirit of revenge or a desire to be a one-man attack on crime because of his father. He held several jobs before deciding to join up in January 1962. "I knew well what the life was like and I decided it was for me," said Sinclair. He moved up through the ranks from constable (when a probationer's pay was $255 a month) to detective sergeant to staff sergeant, and then became an inspector for twelve years, working mostly on organized crime. He retired in 1997. He is proud of the 50 years between them that he and his father gave to Vancouver's police department.

Sinclair said he never thought of his father when he walked or ran down a dark alley where there was the probability of meeting armed, desperate crooks in the darkness. He pulled his gun many times during a long career. "You always look around to see who might be in hiding, but there was never time for me to dwell on the past."

He is active in the association of retired policemen, which has about 500 members, and still takes pride in the force, although he smiles ruefully as he mentions the police department's penchant in recent years "for seeming to be always shooting itself in the foot." He feels that the procession of chiefs who didn't serve very long for various reasons is a main cause of instability, insecurity, or morale problems that plague the force in 2002. Without wanting to spend too much time in memory lane or to overstress that things aren't what they were in his day, he believes that the concept of the beat bobby, although modernized in part, has been lost. Sinclair says he thinks a downside to hiring new recruits with various university degrees is that some "want to sit in offices, battling crime electronically, without having to go out into the streets and the community to meet it head-on at its basic level."

He is extremely proud of his role in the police pipe band in which he and his father devoted so much time and effort. Ian Sinclair was its pipe major for many years and is a well-known performer across Canada. He has also travelled with the band to the United States and overseas. He still has his father's favourite pipes; the bag has rotted, but the rest of it and its silver mountings look as good as new. Sinclair ruefully admits that despite his best efforts he was unable to impart his love of the pipes or Scottish folklore to his children, but he has hopes that one day his small grandson will want to skirl on the old instrument like his grandfather and his great-grandfather.

A Policeman Recalls

Sid Devries was a policeman who played a key role in the quick arrest of Joe Gordon on the night of the killing. The 34-year veteran of the department retired as an inspector in 1982 after spending much of his career on the drug squad. "I started walking a beat on Hastings Street, and I got to know almost all of them involved in the drug racket," he recalled. In the early 1950s Vancouver was a smaller place and the drug business was not as sweeping as it is today. Devries said he was aware that Joe was a well-known crook, but he was not one of his prime considerations. "He came to my notice because he seemed to know all the dealers and hung around with some of them," said the ex-inspector.

Devries said Gordon was not an addict, nor was he involved in the front end of narcotics peddling. He said he always thought of Gordon as an organizer, and if he had any connection with the trade it was at the back end and not visible. Because Gordon at times kept company with the dealers, Devries one day jotted down the licence-plate number of a convertible that he saw Gordon driving.

He was at headquarters the night Sinclair was murdered. "After they found the abandoned car and radioed in the licence-plate number, I was able immediately to connect Gordon with the car," recalled Devries. Also on the police records was an address Gordon was known to visit. Devries joined Lamont and the squad that went to the apartment at 1350 Burrard Street. Devries was the first man into the suite, where they found and arrested Gordon with the brown-paper parcel containing the mud-spattered pants and shoes that were important exhibits in the murder trial.

The justice system proceeded to dispose of Joe Gordon.

EPILOGUE

History documents real-life events and lessons learned the hard way. Joe Gordon's final destiny was to be hung by the neck until dead. His final message suggested that he was a victim of his environment.

Vancouver, British Columbia, is one of the loveliest cities in the world. It is also home to one of the saddest areas in all of Canada: the core of East Hastings Street, now known as "the downtown east side." It's a refuge for a collection of tattered, tormented, and often sick derelicts drawn here from across the country and abroad by Vancouver's moderate climate and a ready supply of drugs. The streets abound with drug dealers and addicts of one kind or another, sniffing cocaine, taking methamphetamine, shooting heroin, drinking cheap booze, and swallowing pills or anything else that comes along in the garbage-strewn alleys. For these unfortunates, as it was 50 years ago with the addict at Joe Gordon's trial, nothing matters but the next fix.

Joe Gordon's Hastings Street was challenging and provocative, and the participants had a kind of "cops and robbers" rapport that was a part of their adversarial relationship. But five decades of decay and a changing social environment have taken a toll. The first few blocks of East Hastings Street have deteriorated so far that the neighbourhood has become a deadly no-man's-land. Today, a beat cop with the Vancouver Police Department would never venture alone into most of Joe Gordon's old territory.

To date, all attempts to restore, salvage, resurrect, or simply clean up these streets have failed. Social programs intent on helping the addicted and impoverished seem only to have nurtured the status quo. Police work has long been a thankless task at the corner of Hastings and Main, with politicians floundering miles away at City Hall.

Since it was formed in 1859, with its headquarters in nearby pioneer Gastown, Vancouver's police force has come under attack from many directions. Residents have frequently blamed it for most of the city's woes. Sometimes they were right, but often they were wrong. Several police chiefs were less than honest, some were incompetent, and a few were both. Chief Walter Mulligan was by far the worst performer, although he had some good points. He introduced new ideas, and he was a persuasive and polished speaker, regarded across Canada as an expert in his field. Unfortunately, he was also a crook. He garnered unwanted headlines for Vancouver across North America when, after seven months of hearings, the Tupper Royal Commission reported to the British Columbia legislature that Mulligan was "capable but corrupt." Newspaper headlines screamed: "Mulligan Discharged" and "Mulligan Got Graft." Mulligan fled to California before he could be charged, where he became a bus driver for a tour company.

Fortunately, his replacement was a man now said by many to have been the best chief ever—veteran RCMP Superintendent George Archer. A ramrod-straight, no-nonsense disciplinarian, he was also a man liked by all. He had modern policing views and took no guff from either the city fathers, who were thankful to get him, or from the demoralized department's usually feisty union. Its members knew better than to complain: They had helped to oust Mulligan because he had leapfrogged into the chief's position while more senior, long-term men were overlooked, but now they knew it was time to rebuild the force.

Although Vancouver's recent police chiefs bear no resemblance to Walter Mulligan, the fact that there have been four different ones between 1993 and 2003 has done little for the stability of the department, which during this period has borne the brunt of public outrage about conditions along skid row. Without stable, predictable leadership, it is difficult for police officers to perform well under fire, especially when they are dealing with a staggering array of violent crime, as well as one of the worst serial-murder cases in Canadian history.[4]

Chiefs have come and gone for various reasons, in rapid succession. William Marshall resigned in 1993 after a provincial inquiry into the treatment of a prisoner in the city jail. He didn't mistreat the prisoner, but one of his men did, and he knew about it. He was replaced by Ray Canuel, a veteran cop who was nearing retirement and never expected to get the job, but, in what was basically a fill-in position, performed well until he was pensioned in 1997.

Then came Bruce Chambers, a man with 30 years' experience and three university degrees. Those who predicted trouble for him were right. He came from Thunder Bay, Ontario, and that fact alone put two strikes against him. Some locals considered it an insult for a man from such a small backwater, as they saw it, to be given a big-city job. Other Vancouver veterans objected strongly to an outsider rather than a local contender being awarded the position. Chambers ran into lots of opposition, both overt and covert. When this hostility was combined with some of Chambers' own actions, it was strike three, and his three-year contract was bought out before it expired.

In 2003 Chief Jamie Graham, Chambers' successor, became the man in the hot seat, supported at the outset by the civic politicians and facing no noticeable initial hostility from the union, which from its beginnings has been in the major league of militant unions in British Columbia. Graham is a former Mountie, like Archer, as is Vancouver's equally new mayor, Larry Campbell, who chairs the police commission.

Shortly after Campbell was elected mayor in November 2002, Chief Graham gave his support to the mayor's plans for tackling the downtown east side's depressing drug jungle, an initiative launched in 1997 by Campbell's predecessor, Philip Owen. This strategy was a key issue in the civic election. The plan follows what is termed a four-pillar approach: prevention, treatment, enforcement, and harm reduction. Many pundits believe that long-time conservative Mayor Owen forfeited his career when he put his convictions ahead of political allegiance to implement this program. He certainly raised national awareness of the need for change.

The enforcement issue was the first to be addressed when Chief Graham borrowed police officers from other regions so that 50 additional beat cops could walk the streets as a visible presence to deter the drug traffic and violence. A harm-reduction strategy of introducing safe injection sites has also been introduced on a trial basis. Only time will tell if these and other actions come close to improving the situation, but at least they are new, positive moves— moves that have been lacking since Joe Gordon's time.

This area of concentrated drug use is not the only policing problem for the Vancouver Police Department. The challenges to be confronted by police are enormous in a fast-growing city of more than a half-million people, surrounded by an even larger, sprawling hinterland of 34 disputatious municipalities housing about two million residents. Along with seemingly uncontrollable drug problems and escalating violence, the police have to deal with an upsurge in electronic crime, credit-card fraud, money laundering, and even the use of cell phones in riots, whereby criminals tell each other where to find the best unprotected stores and businesses to smash into and loot.

Police personnel are carefully trained for a difficult role; most of them have university degrees. Unlike the untrained force of the 1950s, officers are no longer handed a gun and sent out on the street. Chief Graham has a number of specialized units that deal with key problems. He has 23 community policing offices, cycle squads, and teams with specialized knowledge in areas such as child pornography, criminal harassment, stalking, arson, vehicle theft, domestic violence, and computer crime. There is a "biker" squad, forensic video unit, a youth squad, a marijuana grow-busters unit, and victim services unit. New specialties evolve on a regular basis to deal with constantly emerging problems.

Vancouver's police officers today are better educated, better trained, and better paid than ever before, but as former inspector Ian

Sinclair pointed out, they still have a tendency to "shoot themselves in the foot." Dealing with aggressive violence, they often appear to be too tough or to use too much force in apprehending suspects. The modern style of journalism ensures that the anomaly of the "rotten apple" gains headlines while the remainder of the barrel is rarely recognized. Chief Graham has said, "We live in a violent world." This means that when a police officer approaches a man who resists arrest and is known to have dozens of convictions against him, force will be used to subdue him if necessary. But when force is used, it is carefully scrutinized by both the press and the justice system.

Today, roving television professionals and a host of amateur video photographers capture every event, exposing to public view a great deal more of the seamy side of things than was seen even a decade ago. Most people are now very much aware via the news of the daily deaths, arrests, and drug busts, but they seldom see the solutions and they believe there is a generally escalating level of violence in the community.

In this media-savvy, multicultural age, Vancouver's police, like those in Toronto, San Francisco, Seattle, and a hundred other cities, have to step carefully around the issue of racism. There are people who have come to North America from violence-prone societies. Some have brought intolerance with them. In Vancouver, police must deal with a wide range of Central American and Asian gangs who roam the alleys off East Hastings Street, making money off drugs and willing to use any means to escape capture.

Although their plans are not made public, law-enforcement officials are giving more attention to the issue of terrorism since September 11, 2001. More time is also devoted to meetings, discussions, and co-ordinating operations with the RCMP, Canada's spy agency CSIS, and American and even offshore police forces and security services. As a major entry point to Canada by land, air, and sea, Vancouver is a popular destination for bogus refugees, fleeing criminals, drug smugglers, and almost everyone else.

Thirty-one languages are spoken among the 1,100 members of the Vancouver Police Department, which comprises many races and nationalities, as well as 200 female officers. In 1997, 139 of the force's 1,084 members were women. The number of officers continues to increase. One hundred new officers were hired in 1999, 49 in 2000, 55 in 2001, and 90 in 2002; Chief Graham hoped to hire another 120 in 2003. These are all positive signs. The new recruits replace retiring officers and provide much-needed manpower and new expertise for the specialized units.

A growing police force is costly, however. In 2003 the police budget was $128 million, up from $104 million in 1997. A rookie constable earns $40,000 a year and an officer with twenty years' service gets $70,586. The rank of staff sergeant has been eliminated, and in 2000 B.C. Corrections took over the role of custodial guards. Chief Graham is the best paid ever, at about $200,000 per annum.

Joe Gordon would not recognize his old neighbourhood; he wouldn't feel at home there anymore, and his smart suits and jaunty wide-brimmed hat would be entirely out of place. He would undoubtedly wish that those who read his letter had paid more attention to his heartfelt request and done more to help the children of his time.

In view of the terrible degradation and decay that have occurred along Hastings since he wrote his final letter, Gordon's words are an apt reminder of how devastating a social environment can be. No one today ends up on the gallows at the end of a rope as Joe Gordon did, but there are many individuals who follow the same pattern of arrest, conviction, incarceration, and release that he did, and the sequence becomes a way of life that seems little better than the gallows—death just takes longer. Only in some cases do the alternatives to a good family life, such as foster care and detention, lead to a more productive lifestyle. Criminals rarely find a way out of this pattern, and there is little initiative for rehabilitation unless all the factors are positive and include such elements as supportive friends or family, a suitable job, preferably a vocation, and a divorce from former criminal acquaintances. That's a difficult formula to put together. The cost is exorbitant and the success rate is low.

In Joe Gordon's day, the rule was "an eye for an eye." Society now offers an alternative, and while Mayor Larry Campbell opines that "no one is disposable," many people would argue that present-day alternatives are more torturous than a quick death. The degradation of the individual who lives like an animal on the streets or is incarcerated behind bars for much of a lifetime is an end akin to death.

Joe Gordon might approve of Vancouver's four-pillar approach if it can keep young people out of jail, the environment in which they learn to be criminals. It seems to offer an alternative to oblivion—and oblivion is indeed something he would never condone.

APPENDIX I:
POLICE FATALITIES

Gordon Sinclair was one of eleven Vancouver policemen shot down, from a total of seventeen who have died in the line of duty, since the department was formed in 1886.[5] They range from a chief constable to a constable, and from men who had served for twenty years to new recruits who had been on the job for only months. Their names and accounts of their deaths are in a special display in the Vancouver Police Museum.

Constable Lewis Byers, at 21 years old, was the youngest to die in the service of his city. A former member of the North West Mounted Police in Winnipeg, he had been with the Vancouver department for only five months when he was killed on March 25, 1912. He was gunned down by a drunk when he responded to a call of shots being fired.

Constable John Lindsay Archibald, aged 27, was shot when he confronted a break-in gang at a Powell Street office on May 28, 1913. Two members of the gang were hanged for his murder.

Constable John McMenomy, aged 22, was electrocuted on November 1, 1913, at the intersection of Cypress and West Eighteenth while he was checking a faulty streetlight.

Detective Richard Levis, aged 28, was killed on August 29, 1914, while he attempted to arrest a suspect in a stabbing. He was felled by the blast from a sawed-off shotgun when he entered the shack where the man was hiding. The killer was hanged.

Chief Constable Malcolm MacLennan, aged 46, was the only Vancouver police chief killed in the line of duty. On March 30, 1917, he chose to lead an assault on a downtown apartment in which a gunman and his girlfriend, both drug addicts, were holed up. The man, an American named Robert Tait, had already fired from a window and killed an eight-year-old boy who had been passing by on the street. Tait committed suicide in the apartment. MacLennan, a popular progressive chief, had appealed unsuccessfully for drug addicts to get medical help rather than jail.

Constable Robert G. MacBeath V.C., aged 24, was a member of the Seaforth Highlanders. MacBeath was eighteen when he won the Victoria Cross for bravery in France in 1917. He was shot and killed at Granville and Davie Streets on October 9, 1922, while trying to arrest an impaired driver who suddenly pulled out a gun. The killer served sixteen years in Canada and then was deported and jailed in the United States.

Constable Ernest Sargent, aged 25, was shot and killed November 10, 1927, while questioning a suspect on the corner of Alder and West Eleventh Avenue. The man was found not guilty.

Constable Joseph Reilly, aged 54, died of injuries December 23, 1932, after the patrol car in which he was riding was involved in an accident at Burrard and Georgia Streets.

Constable Charles Boyes, aged 39, and Constable Oliver Ledingham, aged 40, were both shot and killed February 26, 1947, in a gun battle with three bank-robbery suspects on the False Creek flats. A third policeman was wounded. The suspects, two of whom were teenagers, had been preparing to rob a bank. One died in the gunfight, one was hanged, and the other was found not guilty on appeal, but was later jailed on drug charges.

Constable Gordon Forbes Fraser Sinclair, aged 40, was shot down on December 7, 1955, while investigating a suspected break-in at 1500 West Third. His killer was hanged for murder while a second accused was saved from the gallows and served fifteen years in jail.

Detective Lawrence Short, aged 42, was shot February 9, 1962, while questioning a fraud suspect in a room at the Bayshore Hotel on West Georgia Street. The suspect also killed the hotel assistant manager and wounded a third man. He was sentenced to hang, but the verdict was reduced to life imprisonment. He served time in Canada before being transferred to a jail in the United States.

Reserve Inspector Arthur Trentham, aged 49, was an inspector with the Vancouver Police Reserve unit. He was struck and killed by a car while directing traffic near the Pacific National Exhibition grounds on September 16, 1963. The hit-and-run driver was charged with impaired driving and leaving the scene of an accident.

Constable Larry Esau, aged 23, a former member of the RCMP, was on duty driving a motorcycle on June 29, 1966, near Woodland and East Hastings streets, when a car suddenly pulled out in front of him and he struck it. He died in hospital of his injuries. A recent graduate of the motorcycle training course, he had been named the best driver in his class.

Constable Paul Sanghera, aged 22, was killed in a motor vehicle accident on January 8, 1982, at the corner of Argyle Street and East Fifty-Seventh Avenue. He was standing beside an abandoned car when a truck skidded on the icy street and hit him.

Sergeant Larry Young, aged 40, was killed on February 2, 1987, while trying to arrest a high-level cocaine dealer in an apartment at 3416 West Sixteenth Avenue. Another policeman was wounded in the gun battle and the killer was shot dead. Young, a corporal, was posthumously promoted to sergeant.

The Vancouver City police force has lost no one in recent years, although law-enforcement members in surrounding cities and municipalities have not fared as well. The most recent fatality occurred at an intersection in Richmond in 2002, when a police car was literally sliced in half by another vehicle driven by a teenager involved in an illegal road race.

Members of the Vancouver Police Department have also volunteered for military duty in both world wars, eleven giving their lives for their country. Lost during the First World War were D.A. Morrison, R. McLean, J.W. Kennedy, H.W. Hall, R. Lemon, E. Scarlett, J.M. Watson, J. Elliott, and W. Morrison. J.H. Sutherland and H.A. Smith were killed in the Second World War.

APPENDIX 2:
HANGING IN CANADA

One of John Diefenbaker's many roles before he became prime minister of Canada was as a scrappy defence lawyer and an ardent opponent of the death penalty. Another former prime minister and fellow abolitionist was Brian Mulroney, also a lawyer. He, too, gave many speeches inside and outside the House of Commons, urging an end to hanging. Mulroney was fond of referring to Diefenbaker's views and citing his passionate statements, such as "From my experience at the bar, I say that anyone who says an innocent man cannot go to the gallows is wrong because I know differently. This is more than a matter of conscience although there is that indeed. It is a matter of seeking justice not revenge." Those who opposed capital punishment in Canada in the twentieth century knew well that they were fighting against a majority of people across the country who still favoured the ultimate penalty.

The last men to be executed in this country were pimp Arthur Lucas, who murdered a prostitute, and cop killer Ronald Turpin. They both died in back-to-back hangings on December 11, 1962, in Toronto's Don Jail while an angry crowd protested outside. The last to die in British Columbia was Leo Anthony Manta in 1959, two years after Joe Gordon, for a stabbing death at the Royal Canadian Navy barracks at Esquimalt, near Victoria. He killed a former homosexual lover.

Execution remained a part of Canadian law for some fourteen years after the last executions were carried out at the Don Jail, but nobody visited the hangman. Although the death-penalty legislation was still in place, the federal government commuted all sentences of death to life in prison. The free vote to wipe the penalty from the law books was narrowly carried on July 14, 1976, when Parliament under Liberal prime minister Pierre Elliot Trudeau voted 130 to 124 in favour. Pro-penalty forces vigorously continued their campaign for the reintroduction of the death penalty, contending that Parliament in 1976 went against the majority opinion of Canadians. Polls showed that this was in fact the case. The retentionists were successful in forcing another parliamentary vote on the contentious question that continued to carve deep emotional divisions in the land. The margin was slightly larger this time, however, when 148 voted to ban the death penalty and 127 voted for retention on June 30, 1987. This second vote came under the Conservative government of Prime Minister Brian Mulroney.

Since Canada's beginning in 1867, abolitionists have called for an end to killing by the state, arguing that the threat of execution is not a deterrent to murder. They frequently cite the example of nineteenth-century England, when crowds who flocked to watch the public hangings of pickpockets had their pockets picked. Thieves had taken their chances within sight of men dangling by the neck.

More recently, critics point out that the United States, the last western country that still puts criminals to death, has a much higher murder rate than countries in which capital punishment has been abolished. Polls in Canada show that support for the death penalty has slipped, with public opinion being about evenly divided. This is a sharp increase in support for abolition from some twenty years ago. Public opinion has been affected by prominent cases in which men jailed for murder were found by DNA sampling and other new scientific investigation to be innocent. Without a change in the law, Donald Marshal and several others could have died on the gallows for crimes they did not commit.

About the time of Gordon Sinclair's murder in 1955, John Diefenbaker came to Vancouver to fight the second trial of a young man who had been sentenced to die for the murder of a Chinese grocery-store owner. On appeal, the accused had been granted a new hearing. In a fiery defence that had the Saskatchewan lawyer and member of Parliament down on the courtroom floor, demonstrating what actually happened during the botched robbery, Diefenbaker won a jury verdict of manslaughter. Many felt he was a much better lawyer than a prime minister, but, of course, this could also be said of others.

In his book *They Were Hanged*, author Alan Hustak[6] states that studies show there are four main arguments in favour of execution: religious beliefs, political policies, sociological factors, and vengeance. He adds that less than a third of the death sentences originally handed down by Canadian courts were ever carried out. Hustak points out that unless executions are conducted in public, rather than before small groups of witnesses in the dead of night, as quietly as possible, society doesn't believe that it has the right to take life. This wasn't the case, however, in the 2001 execution of the Oklahoma bomber in the United States, mass killer Timothy McVeigh. He had a large audience of victims' relatives watching in person as well as on closed-circuit television.

Hustak lists some of the ghastly happenings at hangings, from an accused who had to be hauled back up and dropped again when he didn't die on the first attempt to a woman who was decapitated at Bordeaux Jail in 1935 when the hangman underestimated her weight by 30 pounds. Another woman was left hanging for an hour and ten minutes before finally being pronounced dead. The last woman executed in Canada was Marguerite Pitre in Quebec City, for delivering the bomb that blew up an airliner over the St. Lawrence River in 1951. The bomb-maker's wife was a passenger on the plane; he and another accomplice paid the death penalty for their involvement. Killers come from all strata of society, states Hustak, pointing to one who was sentenced to die while his brother was a justice of the New Brunswick Court of Appeal. The author says that in addition to innocents who were wrongly killed, there have been other cases where the verdict should have been manslaughter, resulting in a jail sentence rather than execution.

Execution has an effect that reaches far beyond the families and friends of the murderers and their victims. Hustak's book cites the tragic case of George Gregory, Victoria war veteran, lawyer, and politician. Gregory defended Leo Manta in an Esquimalt murder case. A former member of the Royal Canadian Navy who had been discharged, Manta climbed the fence at the Esquimalt barracks and stabbed his former lover as he lay in his bunk. They had quarrelled and ended their affair some time earlier. Manta was pronounced dead twelve minutes after the trapdoor opened. After witnessing the hanging, Gregory later wrote: "We all know how Leo died but not how he struggled, which may have been such that his end is justified and accepted by God." A former partner of Gregory's said the execution had greatly affected the former member of the Legislature, who had become more emotionally involved in the case than in any of the many others he handled.

In 2001 a Canadian judicial decision stated that two young British Columbia men wanted in Washington State for a triple murder would not be returned to the United States unless the judiciary there promised they would not be subject to execution. The American authorities somewhat reluctantly agreed. Such decisions are occurring with increasing regularity. In the view of many experts, this fact rules out the chances of the dwindling number of pro-death-penalty believers ever having their wishes restored in Canadian law.

ENDNOTES

1. For a complete portrayal of the events surrounding the inquiry, see *The Mulligan Affair* by Ian Macdonald and Betty O'Keefe (Heritage House, 1997).

2. The query was cited as an access request under the Freedom of Information and Protection of Privacy Act. In replying on November 15, 2001 (FOI Number: 01-1466A), Randy Smith, a constable analyst (359) of the Information and Privacy Unit of the Vancouver Police Department, stated: "Please be advised that our search for the records that you have requested has determined that all files from the year 1955 have been destroyed by our archives." Constable Smith added that a request for a review of the department's response could be made to the Office of the Information and Privacy Commissioner in Victoria. The authors sent a letter to the commissioner, asking if it was normal procedure for such material to be destroyed and what were the rules governing these actions, particularly the length of time material was to be held before it could be shredded. They received this answer: "There is no space to retain anything beyond seven years."

3. This money was in addition to the Crown-paid lawyers' fees for the accused.

4. In spring 2002, after some pressure from the public, the police launched an investigation to determine the fate of 60 women who had disappeared from the downtown east side since the 1980s. DNA sampling identified the remains of fifteen of these women, found at a pig farm in Port Coquitlam, B.C. Robert Willie Pickton, part owner of the farm, has been charged with fifteen counts of murder. At the time of this book's printing, the investigation of the farm and of other sites was continuing, and Pickton's trial date had not yet been set.

5. The information for the appendix was drawn from Joe Swan's *A Century of Service—The Vancouver Police, 1886-1986*, published in 1986 by the Vancouver Police Historical Society and Centennial Museum.

6. Alan Hustak, *They Were Hanged* (Toronto: J. Lorimer, 1987).

REFERENCES

Primary Sources
Vancouver Public Library

Books
Hustak, Alan. *They Were Hanged.* Toronto: J. Lorimer, 1987.
Swan, Joe. *A Century of Service—The Vancouver Police 1886-1986.*
    Vancouver: Vancouver Police Historical Society and Centennial
    Museum, 1986.

Newspapers
Vancouver Daily Sun
The Daily Province, Vancouver
Vancouver News Herald
New Westminster Columbian
Victoria Colonist
Victoria Times

PHOTO CREDITS

Bill Dennett/*Vancouver Sun*: Cover photo and 86
Ian Sinclair: 37, 38, 59
Stewart McMorran: 52
Vancouver City Archives: 85
Vancouver Public Library: 20, 56
Vancouver Sun: 61, 76, 86, 134, 149

INDEX

Also by Ian Macdonald and Betty O'Keefe

ISBN 1-895811-45-7
$16.95

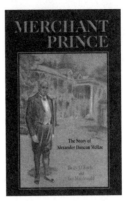

ISBN 1-894384-30-X
$18.95

ISBN 1-895811-96-1
$16.95

ISBN 1-895811-64-3
$16.95

ISBN 1-895811-11-3
$17.95

Heritage House

Phone: 1-800-665-3302 Fax: 1-800-566-3336

Visit our website
www.heritagehouse.ca

Betty O'Keefe was a Vancouver *Province* reporter for seven years in the 1950s. She later worked as a weekly-newspaper editor, a public relations consultant, and a communications supervisor. In 1994, she resigned as executive director of the Employee Share Ownership and Investment Association to embark on a writing partnership with Ian Macdonald.

Ian Macdonald joined the *Vancouver Sun* after stints at the Victoria *Times Colonist* and the *Vancouver Province*. He was the *Sun*'s legislative reporter in Victoria for five years and bureau chief in Ottawa from 1965 to 1970. He worked in media relations for the prime minister's office and was head of Transport Canada Information. He has written for magazines, radio, television, and film.

Macdonald and O'Keefe's books on West Coast history include *The Mulligan Affair: Top Cop on the Take* (1997), which was nominated for the City of Vancouver Book Award, *The Sommers Scandal* (1999), *The Final Voyage of the Princess Sophia* (1998), *Canadian Holy War* (2000), and *Merchant Prince* (2001). Their next project, *Dr. Fred and the Spanish Lady*, is a book about the Spanish flu epidemic of 1918, and will be published by Heritage House in 2004.